Crito
Di
Volta

an epic

ESSENTIAL POETS SERIES 275

Guernica Editions Inc. acknowledges the support of
the Canada Council for the Arts and the Ontario Arts Council.
The Ontario Arts Council is an agency of the Government of Ontario.
We acknowledge the financial support of the Government of Canada.

MARC DI SAVERIO

Crito
Di
Volta
an epic

GUERNICA
EDITIONS

TORONTO • BUFFALO • LANCASTER (U.K.)
2020

Anna van Valkenburg, editor
Michael Mirolla, general editor
Cover and interior design: Rafael Chimicatti
Cover image: Тоталитарная архитектура, Розанов Михаил
(Wikimedia Commons)
Guernica Editions Inc.
287 Templemead Drive, Hamilton, (ON), Canada L8W 2W4
2250 Military Road, Tonawanda, N.Y. 14150-6000 U.S.A.
www.guernicaeditions.com

Distributors:
Independent Publishers Group (IPG),
600 N. Pulaski Road, Chicago, IL 60624, U.S.A
University of Toronto Press Distribution (UTP),
5201 Dufferin Street, Toronto (ON), Canada M3H 5T8
Gazelle Book Services, White Cross Mills
High Town, Lancaster LA1 4XS U.K.

First edition.
Printed in Canada.

Legal Deposit – First Quarter
Library of Congress Catalog Card Number: 2019947116
Library and Archives Canada Cataloguing in Publication
Title: Crito di Volta : an epic / Marc Di Saverio.
Names: Di Saverio, Marc, author.
Series: Essential poets ; 275.
Description: Series statement: Essential poets series ; 275
Identifiers: Canadiana 2019016025X | ISBN 9781771835213
(softcover)
Classification: LCC PS8607.I235 C75 2020 | DDC C811/.6—dc23

for MICHELLE FABRIS,
the Muse of these verses.

Michelle Fabris (1971-2018) was a Canadian civil rights leader who championed, defended, comforted and empowered the ill and the homeless—they were closest to her heart—despite her own enormous and exhausting health struggles. Michelle Fabris possessed the valour of William Wallace and the elegance of Anna Pavlova. Michelle Fabris taught me that bravery does not mean to be fearless in the face of danger; it means to be frightened in the face of danger, yet to engage that danger, nevertheless. Michelle Fabris taught me how to fight any peril, despite my anxieties; how to steadfastly strive to be bold in order to stay true—despite the fear and despite the consequences. With the exception of the Almighty Himself, Michelle Fabris inspired and continues to inspire me more than any force on earth.

Michelle Fabris, my leader, my touchstone, my comrade, my love: rest in joyful peace, forever.

Contents

Leave Him alone; don't you fear God,
even when you are dying?
— New Testament

I. A Letter to Flavia Vamorri

from: Crito Di Volta <patient.power@gmail.com>

to: Flavia Vamorri <bakuninite.2000@gmail.com>

I.

(on a weekend pass)

Flavia, my eyes are red as the sunrise this first time I swallow
   my speed and hope …

Teetering on the street like a bull full of swords, the sunbeams
   stabbed me while wishes to see you staggered me across to
   the Diplomatico, where, calvaried in the laughter of the
   patio, hunchbacked in misfitness, I saw your sword-splitting
   eye-light boil my wounds into a moment of balm.

May you always be the dandelion growing into blows of
   perpetual steps, and never the iris growing into passive
   opulence.

May you never be taken until completely given …

A crow alights the spire-point in the snow while this patient
   tries to try to believe the father's promise of "ray-straight"
   reasons up God's sleeve.

The father—

a lonesomeness snakes through his quavering veins and
   lotus-skinned, soleness-cored soul.

I turn …

Out from the dying echoes of his howls I crisply sing The
  Smiths through the streets, gallivanting free—
Flavia, the amphetamine's working!
… After the T.M.S and the E.C.T, after the Clozapine and
  the exorcizing, after years of pitch darkness with an
  autumn wasp, after the Sanatoriums and the psych ward
  queens who snuffed themselves despite having sworn on
  my soul they would never, and who did not leave a note
  behind—I feel like a Romantic, again …
Flavia, be in me as the strength of an orphan supermanning
  in his sorrows and calamity.
May your heart so naturally dart for the tear-skinned
  wasp-cored souls, but not be stung.
Rattle the world harder than the guerrilla machine-gunning
  at the start of her first battle.
Be in me as the brusque verity of a cadaver, and not as
  anything hazy: an Afghan field of poppies for the
  unrequited lover.
Have me in the intensity of Christ on the cross, a second before
  he gave, and not in the calm comfort of a lover in my arms.
Let us to the prisoners of war who'll hang themselves, and not
  to the easy chit-chat of drunk inheritor-dandies …
I won't let you be taken until completely given …
Would you rather be the speed of a sunbeam or its brightness?
Have me in the holy lunacy of maniacs on soapboxes in
  city-cores and college borders, blasting manifestoes, and
  singing the melody-lines of people's veins …
Flavia, when we met at Diplomatico I never wore my
  contacts so I could look you in the eyes …
Now I go forward with foot-soles of wind …
Flavia, don't let me be taken until completely given.

II.

Before our Santa Clara or Coup D'Amore,
before Overpoetry or Götterdämmerung,
before we become comrades and write
manifestoes and propaganda of light,
before the Kingdom is sparked by the swords' clash
or bullet ricochet, before we have been sung,
before we smash and re-map and dash
and shoot out in the star-white snow on the More-
sure shore of the bull's-eye of peace, hit with a bullet ...
let's become lovers; let's drive through Rome
then take a scenic road through my father's home-
town in Abruzzo; let's get
mangoes, Prosecco, Muratti's, and speed;
let's write love sonnets first, *then* the new age's creed!

III.

The phoenixes of our spirits cling
claws above the deluge as we dalliance;
with weak wings I rest a moment against you
in flight, talons loosing. Through mirrored veers
and ardour-softened beaks' sweetest
meetings, we soar toward theophanies.
The phoenixes of our spirits live on dew.
With four beating wings of fire we
rapturously sing like Orpheus to

Eurydice during their courtship,
and, all the other animals
silence—magnetized, stronger, dazzled.
The phoenixes of our spirits will sign
the wind with charisma high-lit in shine!

IV.

Let's go to the Sanatorium's One Hundred And Twenty-Fifth
    Anniversary Summer Solstice Dance, where the patients'
    auras mingle into proto-palpabilities.
Let's breathe the afflatus of the 'manics.'
Let's dance the steps of the 'schizophrenics,' channelling a
    music we will never hear.
Let's share our cigarettes, pot, and beer; while they share the
    light that's gone out in the world.
The Sanatorium, where the best minds of our time share no
    majestic court, and steer Mankind despite its shame of
    them.

(((O)))

Crito

II. A Letter to Niccolo Di Volta

from: Crito Di Volta <patient.power@gmail.com>

to: Niccolo Di Volta <venetian.boat.song@gmail.com>

I.

Dear Niccolo:

I know how hard to visit here can be; thank you for coming,
thanks for the presents ...

Last week I took my first Amphetamine; it worked just minutes
after consumption! I'm getting released later this week...

Today I sold three oils for thirty g's; now I'm going to live
spontaneously.

Do send me your rendition of "Raindrop." May your weekend
be a whirlwind of gold.

Training myself to speak in five-foot lines (hence this pentametric
letter, bros.)

These reflect what we said in the courtyard:

II. *Jesus and Judas*

    for Niccolo Di Volta

And now the Feast of Unleavened Bread drew near
and Judas practiced kissing on his hand
and Jesus prayed and cheered a passing band
of fiery-eyed foreseers without fear,
setting on its way again, like the sun,
blazing forth now, letting Jesus steer
it with trails of greenery that even
stunned the last-born baby of the mere
caravan. He turned the rocks
to streams that rushed, then flowered
the deserts ahead of these roamers free to endure
their familiar empire's gloomy future.
And as Jesus unlocked his eyes with Iscariot,
He was arrested, blasting: ramble on!

III. *Standing on Opposite Sides of the Stream*

    for Niccolo Di Volta

Standing on opposite sides of the stream dividing the ravine—
    you singing verses and I singing choruses, then vice-versa;
    the spring stream thin; the kindred ravine dimming; mom
    biting her first nail on the phone with Aunt Josie; dad
    inside the study, reciting Leopardi; both at home.

Standing on opposite sides of the stream dividing the ravine—
   you practicing your curve-balls, I catching all your curve-
   balls; we synchronized brothers with same-sized shadows,
   equal in our gifts; the strongest want each having for the
   other being that the other would out-bloom, out-explode
   him, like one cherry-blossom might out-bloom, out-explode
   another—
Standing on opposite sides of the stream dividing the
   ravine—you praying to Saint Cecile, I praying to Saint
   Cecile; the cardinals, camouflaged by the late red rays,
   seeming to shoot out of nowhere, out of the vortex to the
   reason for coincidence, the Stranger's way of remaining
   anonymous?
And, soon, telling the time by the fainting sun, I'd jump
   the stream.
And, now, I remember that holy moment when we saw how
   beauteous it'd really be, to enter our paradisal home
   before our father—in his white undershirt, young still,
   glowing unlike the sun at the ends of those evenings—
   had set out toward us.

———

Phone me after the weekend, mang!

Crito

III. New Year's

For Ezra Pound (1885-1972)

Convalescenza, Ezra;
after ten years my
lightning-white blooms of charisma
return, intoxicating mates
who did not spurn me
when I turned into a blight of black tirade.

Plotting in
the garret ...
Now I will bear your contempt of oppressors—
now I will resuscitate the sublime in the old sense,
making new my pursuit
of liquidating Pomo.

When I soon visit
L'Isola di San Michele
I'll sing you the future of newness with a lute
and atomize your infamy with lasers of my lines—
I'll bribe the grave-diggers with our songs
to let me lie by you till dawn.

A wind of ash
blasts four power chords of Vivaldi through my chimes
and ascends me the scent of lily-of-the-valley
from Ricky *Rapallo's* funeral home,

amid aurora borealis! Coincidences?!
You're alive as I this godly New Year's Eve!

    I orate my mates
with a river of rushing bedrocks. Which poltroonish
lyrical anaemic will be the lamp-light of civilization
in the sixty-year-old darkness? See? See!
    Which MFA professors do not spread
    poltroonish lyrical anaemia? O postmodernity!

    Like lightning
  from a snow-cloud
      you shocked the Lost then lit their way
  and struck all sorts of mortmain. Sublimely
impossible, you realized everyone's dream,
    and your errors were extensions of magnanimity.

    For each second counted down,
I see a face of a friend still locked in
Sanatorium, too blinded by frenzy to be the born seer
my worldly friends cannot be ... Two, one—
    a Roman candle's blasted from my window
    into a snow-fort ... I tell my mates to go, now.

The new wood broke
and you carved it into a long knife,
      which I have cast in steel to bleed
    passivity and tyranny.
        In The Emergency Present,
    my pen is my hand, my knife is my other.

Like the street-stones
during a parade, some minds are disturbed
continually, no one knowing or caring;
        I wonder if Charon will ask these transients for coins
or speak to them the first soft words they'll hear since they were
        kids.

        After ten years of institutionalization,
                wonder trumps all:
the verve of the variable wind, the sublimely unsingable
        chimes, the mobocracies of snow and freezing rain
        and the protean balance of passers-by
                excite me like the spring's first lightning.

        Children with their
wooden swords and water-guns and snowball crates
        rive for two forts; the Roman
        candle damage now amended by the freezing rain,
                which solidified both strongholds—
the no-man's land reflecting a red salamander-cirrus.

        One fort overshadows the other.
A long-haired boy in a star-white trench coat fires the first
        snowball, which explodes into a rainbow of paint
across the loftier forts façade. Now, a trinity
        of stone-cored snowballs cracks the rainbowed face …
                Still, no counterattacks.

        … I fell asleep in Toronto's metro and dreamt
I was gondoliering to L'isola di San Michele,
with a stone in my shoe …

I found you standing on your grave,
maybe 22, eating roses … We got into the gondola
and rowed toward your apartment in the dawn.

IV. A Letter from Flavia Vamorri

from: | Flavia Vamorri *<bakuninite.2000@gmail.com>*

to: | Crito Di Volta *<patient.power@gmail.com>*

Breathtaking verses, Crito Di Volta! (An eternity of thank you's; these poems are primo.) And I'm s-o-o-o elated to hear the Amphetamine is working! But pairing would mean the end of the Movement! We're the Che and Fidel of the Patients' Rev.! We cannot abandon our people for ourselves!

See you tomorrow for the ... (fingers crossed); your loyalty never fails me. When I have finished my studies in dance, and I'm the best dancer I can be, I am not only going to write you a ballet—I am going to play the lead. I've already begun the first steps!

Again, Crito, breathtaking verses!

Your comrade,

Flavia

V. Psych

A girl uncrosses her legs, quaveringly. She plays with a
clothespin clipped onto her skirt, near whose hem a white
cross over-laps the verdant shades that intersect to form a
chequered pattern. Her long blonde locks, seized with hair
spray, hang like the boughs of a Weeping Willow after an ice
storm. She removes her fitted yellow jacket. Her off-white
turtleneck reads SAINT JOAN OF ARC HIGH SCHOOL
across the chest. "I dunno if I can tell you what I think I
need to tell you," she says, "but I really want to, you know?
I'm just, like, afraid, to be honest. I've never told anyone
about this … It's only been three times I've been here, and,
and it matters to me what you think of me, and, and I've got
this likely foolish fear you'll surely think less of me if I say
what really, truly, occupies so much of my mind all the time
…" She crosses her legs, pointing her toes toward Doctor
Lesley; he strokes his beard a few times. "Before we
continue," starts Lesley, "how did you get that bruise on your
right thigh? …" The girl encircles the bruise with her
forefinger as one might encircle the rim of a wineglass.
The formal light in her eyes half-softens. "So, did you get
that bruise from soccer, or from Marshall?" continues Doctor
Lesley. "From Marshall." A slight excitement fills the doctor's
wide-open eyes. The girl stands up. "I think I have to go …"
"No, no, no! … SIT DOWN—" Doctor Lesley stands,
his blazer mismatching his corduroys. He notions to the girl,
with his hands, to sit down, and she obeys his order. "So,
that time you had a fat lip—it was from Marshall, not from
an older girl at school, not from Julie the bully?" "Yeah, it

was Marshall …" "I'm—I'm *so* sorry I lied to you! …"
The girl tears up. Doctor Lesley hands her a tissue from his
pocket the way a blue blood might hand a scantily clad
beggar-girl a twenty-dollar bill, to virtue-signal bystanders.
"Why does he beat you? …" "Well, he rapes me too, and,
and the truth is I, I like the way he treats me. See, he's never
particular about his causes for hurting me which, really, well,
it—it arouses me, makes my life feel dangerously,
wonderfully spontaneous—I can't believe I just said that to
you, but I should tell you more, I really should! I trust you
…" Doctor Lesley whips his head back and looks down
upon the girl. He slightly smiles while she closes her eyes for
a long moment, seemingly savouring a memory. "You should
have seen this bruise last week, Doctor Lesley. It's not much
of a bruise now, but it will always be so dear to my memory."
"Did you ever get raped earlier in your childhood?" The girl
looks downward: "Yes …" "More than once?" … "Yes."
Doctor Lesley's eyes appear even hungrier now; the girl
begins to weep, uncrossing her legs, then crossing them
the other way. "Sometimes, but not always, girls who are
repeatedly raped early in life, seek bad partners, and they,
in time, develop their tastes by force. They go from dreading
and loathing the rape, the beatings, to accepting, and even
loving them. So, if rape and violence are consensual, it *can* be
healthy, even …" "But there's more I have to tell you, much
more, and it doesn't feel healthy at all …" Doctor Lesley
loosens his tie, then undoes the top button of his shirt. He
closes a window. "Tell me more. I'm listening." The girl looks
into the doctor's eyes, blinklessly. "Listen," the girl begins,
"I think I'm in love with you! Like, I think about you all the
time, and I don't think I've ever been so attracted to a man in

all my life, and it makes me feel vulnerable and confused—desperate even." The girl uncrosses her legs yet again and looks into Doctor Lesley's eyes. She, once again, encircles the bruise on her thigh with an index finger, all the while maintaining eye contact with the young doctor. "Do you think I'm beautiful?" "Yes, I do," assures the doctor. "And everything right now feels okay, and it's okay, right?" "Yes." "Then why are you sitting so far from me?" Doctor Lesley rises from behind his desk, his phallus erect and exposed: "Come here." "Wait. I have a better plan," replies the girl, "rather than risk getting caught in here, why don't you meet me outside the Fontbonne Building in fifteen minutes; then we can find an hotel ... it would be safer for you, and, plus, your office is about as warm as an Egyptian tomb." "-kay; fifteen minutes, outside Fontbonne." The girl prepares to leave the office. It's nearing five o'clock. Doctor Lesley begins to pack his suitcase as the girl begins to exit the office, "One more thing," she begins, "does the name Chelsea Swan sound familiar, or did you forget her after being found not guilty of statutorily raping her in this very office?! Or did you forget her after she hung herself on account of your deforming her mind, absolutely?! ... By the way, dumb-dumb, I don't have a boyfriend, and I've never been raped, and those bruises were fake, you—you fuck—You, You! And all I said were lies, and all that was an act, you, you reprobate! Maledetto! Ma-le-de-tto!" Officers enter. Flavia exits the office with tears flowing down the SAINT JOAN OF ARC lettering upon her turtle neck. She removes her big blonde wig as she runs toward me, revealing her short red hair; we embrace. One of the officers presses play on an iPhone: "I dunno if I can tell you what I think I need to tell you, but I really want to, you know? I'm just, like, afraid, to be honest. I've never told anyone about this … It's only been three times I've been here, and, and it matters to me what you think of me, and, and I've got this likely foolish fear you'll surely think less of me if I say what really, truly, occupies so much of my mind all the time …" "We were tracking your whole 'doctor' appointment in the waiting room." The doctor weeps with his head down, and with his eyes closed. Poor Flav; she was Chelsea's roommate once, on Ward Seventeen.

VI. Prelude to the Overpoet

At Flavia's attic party, I popped two caps
of E that must have been cut with LSD …
Lips of worms kiss me while the wind slaps
the green out of the spruces and the stoplights.

My eyes, now blue-winged butterflies, tirelessly
beat themselves into caresses for the invisible,
who sing Leopardi's *A Se Stesso* in Greek,
as syllables pop into signals when I speak.

While epiphanies street-fight over me
I bet the sun my eye-lights for its rays
that these will be my most visionary
days, that my vortex of utopia will craze

all humans attempting to see
beyond what they can see through their malaise.
I wear my visions on my sleeve and heart-
beat Suicide to death, and seduce

the tyrants with my hung tongue (and reduce
the Vatican?). A tilt of my head eclipses the sun,
whose ring I propose to everyone.
The Overpoet will survive the "poets'" noose

of slack, finally, after all the years of jeers,
which hunchbacked his spirit like Keats' critics.
Why do the "poets" always mock the seers
and laugh at vatic voices? A vatic voice,

like a spokes-poking stick, will hurl the Dada-rider
skyward then down to the jetty of his mind;
and the Overpoet, an outsider,
will lead his jeerers first, then humankind.

VII. Il Mortarista

(on my twenty-seventh birthday)

I. *Il Mortaio*

"Like a lone vermillion pillar marking oases in a desert,
    he stands!" mocks a professor.
I blast upon the sky-blue tabletop with hand on hip.
"What are you doing up there?" a student jeers.
What are you doing down there*!* I sear.
I'll split your brain in half with my tongue if I must, but trust
    I wish for peace the most!

We sleep under the microscope of those who bloom in the shadows!
We must *wake soon or sleep unto our deaths—*
exist *beneath the microscope of those who live in the shadows?!*
Unite, uprise, or sleep unto our deaths!

You who've never mourned in private chambers,
nor learned the ways of penitence,
nor cared enough to think to learn,
nor thought enough to learn to care—
I've come to you for outdoor celebrations,
I've come to you for your libations to cascade the rising insights
    of my end-time epiphanies.
And you who've never raised the standards of your spirits—
let me brace your forearms so they'll withstand the weight of
    nothingness, and then the weight of the universe.

And you who've yet to unwrap your minds of firm-woven
    false-flags—I will do your thinking for you till your minds
    are naked in the truth-light, again.
And you inside the safety of your -isms, you who can only thrive
    in-side the ivoriest of ivory towers, who may only be beloved
    among one sort of people—
I will teach you danger and risk, again.
I will teach you how to address the masses you hate, and who
    probably hate you,
then teach you how to love the masses; or, wait, the former after
    the latter—I almost had you.
You who are rich, even, but have gardeners and no friends.
You who've grown too keen on stasis.
You who've sought out campy pamphlets on how to become a
    heroin addict—
I'll cast out your demons at your commands,
I'll bend your browning spoons without my hands.
You who love memes with nativity scenes of Lego-blocks or Plasticine—
I will show you;
I will teach you the family, again.
And you who histrionically attempt your acts of warmth in this
    Age of Ice, just so you might claim your own humanity?
I will teach you to be natural, again; then human, again; then
    godly, again; okay?
O, now, listen, know:
this is a prayer, this is a prayer, and I am praying now!
this is a prayer, this is a prayer; you're in a temple now!
You who've not yet distinguished the feeling of dew from sweat
    upon your high, light brows,
take thought: I sing and pray these preludes, these east-lit words, these
    letters of secrets I set to my off-beating heart, for you, too:

We must wake soon or sleep unto our deaths;
must cast the first stones at Horus' eye;
must seek his world's hiding human chiefs,
whose gray waves break like their promises to us—
break over bells of a church, where choruses die.
How will we cross the fading white horizon
when we are all entranced by their wave-lengths?
Should we now dress in black for both of us?
We must wake soon or sleep unto our deaths!

We must wake soon or sleep unto our deaths;
might see streets lit with bankster-torches; mustn't
side-walk our heritage on garbage day; must
learn, once more, the way to the Temple,
for there is One who knows the way to our door
and below the vulture-gyre above the shore
their gray waves break like their promises to us,
the horizon is bearing the sky like a truss.
We must wake soon or sleep unto our deaths!

We must wake soon or sleep unto our deaths,
must thrust our souls of swords into the shadows,
no matter who our hidden masters be,
under whose microscopes we sleep in stabbing light,
under whom we cheerlead the destruction of our kind—
our heads bowed down with the weight of the media
like a new dawn's dew-heavy daisies. Sideway
waves of dandelion clocks will whirl up to the heavens.
We must wake soon or sleep unto our deaths …

"Why do you sing every word you project?!" a poet incites.

I do not sing my verse so I'll be sung louder than the poets who
can only recite, but sing to draw the youth who forever might
not care for unsung verse; who, rather, tell their friends of the
poet who sings *so well —a poem must be sung to be heard by*
the universe.

And I balk at nothing—not nothingness nor treachery, nor
assassins nor Sheol—and give you my life, as well as my
verse, to pay the people the poets' ancient toll.

I see Niccolo pleading with the guards like a father might
plead for the life of his child—
O my baby brother.

You try to force me into wolf's clothing, but I stand here with
my bare soul before you.

O LET ME BEAM THE LOVE FOR YOU I AM!

Inside the knee-jerk glowers of the guards, I see a nearly
palpable softness.

The crowd expands like an horizon line
sprawled before a teenaged boy
standing at the Mountain brow
gazing beyond the falcon gyres.

Mortar:

v. 1. to bombard and destroy
n. 2. a cement used in building

Take my MORTAIO,
my MALTA E PIETRA!

Through the moonless, starless, endless night of Now; with the forth-swinging, blazing, wrecking ball of Mortarism; with the steel cables of our spirits; with the operator of our history lessons; with the crane of our hate for the emergency present— let's demolish the star-stickered, light-blocking ceilings of present Western "Verse," "Art" and "Democracy".

Let's sing an Overpoetry!
Let's bring the first Musocracy!

Let's turn "Art" into a tastefully-dressed, breath-taking, perfectly-proportioned, breath-giving, voluptuous, lactating, ultra magnanimous nurse, with ways-changing, evolution-redirecting milk; an eternal nurse of our sick, degenerating nature.

Let's overthrow those phony poets professing to pliable neophytes: "behold, here is how to leap over poetry's limbo bar and into The Antigonish."

The "verse" of today is lesser than urine since at least urine flows and is not always yellow!

Beware of MFA programming!
Beware of MFA pro-gram-ming!

Beware of MFA programming!
Beware of MFA pro-gram-ming!

Never stifle passion for the sake of a fashion started by the
passionless so they could pass as poets too!
Drivers of their lines of "verse" are failing their beginners' tests,
but "poet"-editor-professors let them graduate with honours, yes!
The "poets" write prose and tailor their "poetics" to their own
inabilities —thereby re-defining poetry as prose—then accuse our
few true poets of not knowing how to write verses at all!
(If only poets spent as much time and energy on poetry-reciting
as they did on poetry-writing; poets seem to think that reciting
poetry comes naturally, without practice!

Perché?
Perché?)

Look, the world is cardiac arresting in a hospice without
doctors!
Poets, we must be cardiopulmonary resuscitation, not a
hospital room painting!
The "poets" write in water rather than ink inside electrical
cages of Political Correctness!
Poetry, you cannot take a forward step on legs of French
philosophies alone!
Canada, I came to you with my soul and with diamonds, and
you tried to collapse them back into a vacuum, back into coal—
Canada, remove your bloody diadem!

(((O)))

If there is no freedom of expression, if there is no freedom of speech, there can be no freedom of State …

O anti-poets, must I Mortaristi storm and fell the Language Police Station of Poetry!?

O anti-poets, strive to be the poets you might have been without the MFA Programming!

O anti-poets, de-program yourselves, then learn the rules of verse before you break them!

O how dismal a sign it is for society, when its poets are passionately pro-censorship!

Does anyone have any water?

A girl wearing a camouflaged shirt passes up some cool spring water to me.

I sip some water, then descend the table.

I stand in the university square, in my good suit, with orphic vigour.

The students divide like the banks of a stream while I wind toward the centre of the crowd.

In the windless, silent square, I exclaim:

A Baphometian Tandem banks on us, string-pulls puppet shows of all its Western Governments; is a potter spinning and moulding the globe with jewelled hands in gloves—our spirits hunchbacked in the impossible pressures of our pitiless masters, against whom we must unite, rather than rive over who is on the left and who is on the right.

We have been divided and conquered in well nigh every
which way—so, unite! Left, right, black, white, man, woman,
atheist, believer, abled, disabled, old, young, Muslim, Christian,
Jew, Gentile, straight, gay, rich, poor, sane, "insane"—Unite!
Let us un-conquer ourselves in the twilight!
Our unity's our masters' greatest fear—
Our masters, who fear we will, in union, overthrow their
ongoing plot to slowly but surely pacify, disarm and enslave us,
to rule us globally, absolutely!
Our unity's our masters' greatest fear—
Our masters, who fear our simultaneous, worldwide
intifadas—behind whom will be the anyway-armed unanimous,
newly awoken, furnace-fiery, furious masses—with blasts of
combat in the streets of the capitals, with broken souls revolting
for the still-wholesome souls of their children!

Now, our love is hard of meeting
as a flame beneath the water,
as a prince's only daughter—
hard of meeting,
yet it was once as easily met
as long-time parted lovers' lips.

If you—like truth—lie in the shadows of Baal,
might take the beast-mark, knowingly or not—
follow my voice till you're out of his veil,

breathe to my breath till you're led from your wail.
If we want, we can reverse our soul-rot.
If you—like truth—lie in the shadows of Baal

yet still can envision light, I will not fail
you; walk beside, not behind me, uncaught.
Follow my voice till you're out of his veil,

follow my voice like the wind does His sail,
follow my voice—it's my own, I'm not bought.
If you—like truth—lie in the shadows of Baal

but still are souled, still try to feel the nail
that Christ eternally feels for you who ought,
follow my voice till you're out of that veil

or never whiff the smoke of your own trail-
blaze, you seeing unbelievers I have sought!
If you—like truth—lie in the shadows of Baal,
follow my voice till you're out of his veil!

I pause to hear the little wind.

It is better to die with nothing but your
soul, than to live with everything but it.

I pause to hear the little wind, again.

(((O)))

O, now, listen, know: under Baphomet and the Unholy
Tandem, the religions of the world will be coagulated into one
demoniacal doctrine, which most of us unknowingly follow,
already—our temples being in our family rooms, before hypnotic
televisions, where we sit on the couches of their sacrificial altars.

(((O)))

And Baphomet, the idol and voice of the Tandem—the leader, whom they worship, for whom they speak—boasts to the Angels of the Universe, in untellable baritones, of his Dominion of Humanity.

And members of the Unholy Tandem may boast:

"Behold the iron hand of my mass media! Behold its gorgeous grip on all those human wills!

"Behold the immeasurable weight of our latest authoritarian pressures, to which all hordes will surely conform, or be shattered like some cheap figurines!

"Behold how predictive our programming is!

"Behold, even the creative thinker, thoroughly de-passionized, fashionably de-aestheticized, through all the MFA Programming, through all the MFA Programming!

"Behold my new technocracy, you serfdoms of humanity!

"Behold the exquisite extent, the immeasurable complexity of my surveillance methods, which may one day make spies go the way of Western bravery!

"Behold all our conformist fools existing in cowardly, comfortable powerlessness, which we have trained them to find desirable, and admirable, even! MUHAHAHAHAHAHAHAH!

"Behold our slaves whose spirits' veins are surely dry as dollar bills, empty as lobotomized prophets.

"Behold how I had, at first, quite subliminally, force-fed; but now, quite obviously, force-feed illegal drugs by enabling a plentiful supply—and enabling the inevitable legalization of these drugs— to weaken, pacify, and demoralize the human will to the point of our own irresistibility, and our slaves' pathetic indifference.

"Behold how I make cadavers of their dreams!

"Behold how the more powerful I become, the less I need to hide!

"Behold me, you masses, you cowards I've made so cowardly!

"Behold the ongoing normalization, accessibility, and even valorization of pornography as 'art,' at first, and then pornography as pornography, at last!

"Behold the fetishization of fetishes!

"Behold the array of racial and sexual revolutions I've hijacked and defiled for the causes of the Tandem, not for the lives of the marginalized minorities! BAHHAHAHAHA!

"Behold how I am introduced to the sleep-working masses as a famed philanthropist and how these zombies believe it!

"Bahhahahahhha!

"Behold this question: do these fools ever even wonder: 'Do we live in a Hypnocracy? Are we all under a mass media-cast spell? Is this conversation even happening, as we sleep-live, as we remain in a static trance?'"

While I catch my breath in the windless square, a girl wearing a blue hijab asks: "What are your thoughts on 9/11, Crito? I was born in Iraq; Iraq was destroyed, and here I am."

I believe that 9/11 was envisioned and blue-printed in the mind's eye of the Devil himself, then orchestrated and eventuated by his evilly wealthy human worshippers, who associate-direct his tragic play of humanity.

The Unholy Tandem played America like Orpheus would an electric guitar. Just as we are under the spell of the Media, the human henchmen who realized 9/11 were under the spell of the Devil; who manipulated them like a mind does a hand, which will pulverize us all unless we fully resist in time! ...

I take a deep breath. I look into the girl's eyes.

I remove my shimmering opal ring. I approach the girl, and place the ring in her hand.

I wore this ring because I believe that opal helps keep one's faith and will strong: here, I want you to have it.

For a moment, she holds onto the ring, which matches her hijab. She slips it over her right forefinger.

O, now, listen, know, I cannot stress enough: I believe it is of utmost importance for gays to have rights, for women to be treated equally, and for blacks and indigenous peoples to be honoured and compensated; but these are not the reasons why so many minority interest groups are either founded by, funded by, or hijacked by the Baphometian Tandem!

And members of the Tandem, I continue, *boast:*

"Behold our control of the means to evolve or devolve human nature at any speed, in any direction, whenever we wish!

"Behold how I hijack noble movements for the downtrodden peoples—sometimes BY the downtrodden peoples—then drive these movements to the point of dividing and conquering portions of the masses, to the point of pathologically creating frictions great enough to ignite and burn both sides of wars, wars, wars, 'the world's hygiene'!

"Behold my promotion of feminism, so as to divide and conquer men and women, so as to sow hatred in women and shame in men.

"Behold my promotion of feminism, so as to ensure mommy is away from the kids, so as to further ensure the Implosion of the Family, so as to isolate your children for long enough periods that the State can raise them—NOT to ensure the equality of women! Bahahhahahhahahh! FOOLS!

"Behold my promotion of gay rights, not because I care for gay lives, but because I care to divide and conquer the homosexual and the heteronormative, to divide and conquer the sexually preferenced!

"Behold, I will hijack and finance black interest groups because I wish to divide and conquer whites and blacks, because I wish to sow hatred within blacks and shame within whites, because I want a fucking race war—NOT because I care for black lives! Muhahahahahah! FOOTSTOOLS!

"Behold, I fund and champion the movements for Aboriginals, not because I care for Indigenous lives, but because I wish to divide and conquer Indigenous peoples and descendants of colonizers; to foster hatred on one side, and guilt upon the other."

"Crito, what nation, what race, are the servants of the Devil?!" a freshman asks.

Just as The Almighty works through the peoples of all races, so too does the Devil, whose immeasurably wealthy human associate-directors live in the long shadows of our struggles—and though we must fight them, we must pray for them. The only one who does not deserve our pity, nor our prayers, nor our forgiveness, is the Devil himself, whose merciless hands wear the black leather gloves of the Tandem, so as not to leave his finger-prints behind, so as not to leave his trace—though the more powerful he becomes, the less he needs to hide, till one day, only the blind will not see him … Anyways, I digress … The Unholy Tandem is interracial, international.

"Behold the Political Correctness with which I have divided and conquered your conversations, closing you into your small talk, alone!

"Behold the Political Correctness we spread—a psycho-spiritual virus, which even snake-spined 'artists' proclaim the religion of all religions!

"Behold how we instil into the repugnant masses, through our many, many means, the belief that conspiracy theories are insane notions of weak-minded people; thus ensuring that so many conspiracy theories do not become truths, far, far faster than we would like—we, who conspire against the masses! MUHAHHAHAHAHAHAHAH.

"Behold forthcoming deportations to tens of empty FEMA camps all silently awaiting dissenters who will not receive the mark of the Beast!

And "Behold!" the Tandemite continues:

"Behold my futurescope—see my world of five hundred million!

"Behold the blueprints of the Khmer Rouge, yet again!

"Behold my baritonic laughter: Muhahahahahahahahaha!

"Behold how scientific endeavours have been, and will be, sabotaged, devaluated, or 'debunked,' except in cases where scientific endeavours are profitable to the Tandem alone.

"Behold how I silence research studies toward affordable or, worse yet, free energy; and how, should a dew-new energy source be found and employed, our vision of exhaustible resources would die, and the extortionist prices of natural fuel would plummet—and that can not happen! Muhahahhahahah!

"Behold my immeasurably worshipable manipulation of crises—or myriad false-flag operations—which will eventuate the precipitation of wars between the First World nations, and our cultivation of starvation and epidemics in the Third World nations!

"*Behold how we delete personal choice, and even Fate, from the human equation, by ceaselessly manufacturing and fostering crises which are all averted or overcome by the authorities, ending yet another need for our own cohesion, our own togetherness!*

"*Behold our formula: Problem, Reaction, Solution, repeat.*

"*Behold the demonic possession of the Hegelian Dialectic! Muhahhahahhhahahah!*

"*Behold how we become mommy, daddy, giver and taker, in one.*

"*Behold how we are mostly takers!*

"*Behold, it's all just so-o-o-o hilarious.*

"*Behold all the war, war, war, the vehicle of all our tenors!*

"*Behold how we either invented, eventuated, or upheld supranational institutions like the League of Nations, the United Nations and the International Monetary Fund, all ungoverned by any higher authority, all above the law, all unanswerable to any nation's peoples!*

"*Behold how we regulate your child's education, collapsing your child's educational aspirations, by adroitly sabotaging the curriculum; behold how, through an "everyone wins" comprehension of sports, we ecstatically enfeeble them further! BAHAHAHHHAHAHAH!*

"*Behold our lust for the sheer decimation of First World economies, which definitely uphold Third World ones; and behold the ensuing calculated tumult, one unlike any before, that will accelerate political disorder and intramural disharmony and violence, whereupon the "only way" to end these complications will be by the unconditional union of all of the earth's governments into one world Totalitarianism!!*

"*MUHAHAHAHHAHAHAHHHHHAHAHHA!*"

Now, what to do?! What to do?!

We sleep under the microscope of those who bloom
  in the shadows!
We must *wake soon or sleep unto our deaths.*
Exist *beneath the microscope of those who live*
  in the shadows?!
Unite, uprise, or sleep unto our deaths!

I see Niccolo in the crowd.
Niccolo-o-o-o-o-o-o-! I ecstatically exclaim like a child
cheering goal.
Some in the audience echo: "Niccol-o-o-o-o-o!" …

… And they shall call for the implantations of microchips in
our right hands!
  And I proclaim this microchip is verily the mark of the Beast!
  And now you know but, still, will you take the mark of the
Beast?!
  And you won't enter Heaven if you take the mark of the Beast!

(((O)))

Why be under the microscope of those who live in the shadows?!
Don't dawns feel goldless as the Fed Reserve?
Don't church-bells toll the death of Christendom?
Is the Pope not an heretical demon?
When will *we learn the Kingdom will not come*
until we unite, with the Nazarene's nerve,
against banksters, puppedents, Bohemian Grove,
one world order under Moloch's thumb?

When John Fitzgerald signed the Holy Order,
his hand was guided by the hand of God.
Go wail at his statue and bow to this martyr!
They'll kill a president who's not a fraud,
who just might try for right, with hallowed gall,
might blood-laud all us to uprise by his fall!

As I take a few breaths and see the phones flashing before me
    like fireflies, I feel a wave of ovation.

I bow like a dew-drooped vermillion tulip.

The full-bloomed fig trees do not move in the weak breeze.

… *It is harder for the unloved to love, so let us love the unloved*
    the most, I think to myself, not knowing why.

II. *Il Mortarista: La Malta E Pietra*

I dream the Amorocracy, one of many bust-jutting saplings I imagined might spring from the seeds of Mortarism, which would be watered by the sweat and blood of the Mortarists. I dream of gli Amoristi, the Amorists, who, in an advanced stage of Mortarism, will struggle to eventuate a society wherein love replaces money as the general currency of a nation, to create a new harmony among the State. Everyone worships money, and takes love for granted; if love were the currency of society, people would worship Love, and money altogether would be nixed.

In the emergency present,
within our quavering souls,
ears of the attics hear
a knocking at their doors …

Now, as afore-wondered: what to do, what to do?

"Let's overthrow the Baphometian Tandem!" yawps a sophomore.

The roar of our spirits being verily voiced echoes through every hall and alley of Mills Memorial Library.

But how? By Might? By Love? By What? And with what will we fill the power-vacuum?

"We'll fill it with Mortarismo!" cries a girl.

Will the force that fills the aforementioned vacuum remain good? Or go bad, like the expired, poisoned milk of postmodernity?

"Crito! You gotta lead the Last Generation to freedom, to victory, to integrity; you must lead us mother-fucked Gen Zedders!" cries a boy.

I step down from the table and stand side by side with other members of the crowd.

I believe I must lead with, not for, and so I stand among you, beside you. I am embraced by the warm wave of students.

O, now, we are quaking in our sleep!
O, now, we are waking from our sleep!

I then re-ascend the table because Niccolo has warned me about radicals of darkness clearly in the square.

Though my body's fading fast, my soul is immolating brightly as the pole star.

O my fellow subsiding serfs: look, see—
we must catch ourselves before we slide away.

(((O)))

One of Adolf Hitler's first orders as Fuhrer was to seize the guns of his citizens. Since learning this, I've been questioning any ruler who wishes to seize his citizens' guns.

First will be the waving of inky wands, not loaded guns; first will be the peaceable strikes; only last might there be violent ones.

I close my weighty lids for one long moment, then tilt my head downward.

"I'm arranging a mic and two amps for you, courtesy of the Music Department. Sit tight and have a sip of water," my brother says.

I take a sip of the cool spring water.

Now, Amos Heine, my best friend, and the young editor who "discovered" me, winds through the crowd toward my soap-box, in his well-worn Leonard Cohen t-shirt. Niccolo, from the opposite direction, also winds toward my soap-box, with one amplifier and one microphone. "We're waiting on the second amp. This way you can save your voice."

As we await the second amplifier, I give a reverential microphone-check of JFK's Secrecy Speech, at first in the voice of JFK, then, eventually, in my own.

I take a long sip of the cool spring water. I hear the crackle of the second amp.

(((O)))

In the Emergency Present, poets should be looking over their shoulders—or else they are doing something wrong, or else they are anti-poets.

In the Emergency Present, poets must not only live by their poems, but even die by them …

I continue on the two-amped microphone, standing upon the sky-blue tabletop:

I can see us, now, setting out to megabanks—together, and never alone, since, I myself, and many others, have already been hounded by them;

I can see us, now, veering toward the state-or-province-owned banks, toward the Credit Union.

I can see us, now, colossally withdrawing from our future bygone banks; and I can see us, now, all listening to Blur's "For Tomorrow," holding onto each other tightly, singing:

"la-la, la-la-la, la-la-la-la-la-la-la-la-la
la-la, la-la-la, la-la-la-la-la-la-la-la-la

la-la, la-la-la, la-la-la-la-la-la-la-la-la
la-la, la-la-la, la-la-la-la-la-la-la-la-la … "

I can see us, now, simultaneously draining daily maximum
amounts from our accounts.

I can see us, together, banking for our bills alone, and holding
onto the rest, as we will be holding onto each other, holding onto
tomorrow, singing:

"la-la, la-la-la, la-la-la-la-la-la-la-la-la
la-la, la-la-la, la-la-la-la-la-la-la-la-la
la-la, la-la-la, la-la-la-la-la-la-la-la-la
la-la, la-la-la, la-la-la-la-la-la-la-la-la … "

I can see us, now, taking our televisions for a walk to the
Mountain Brow, wherefrom we will catapult them—yes, why
shouldn't we build a catapult!—into the massive chasm.

I can see us, now, transforming toward a time when our
bodies will be cleanly temples, with clear sky-lights, so that
soul-light might shine out and the Christ's light might shine in.

A moment slowly passes; a subtle, warm wind caresses
my face.

I notice Flavia in the audience, standing with Niccolo
and Amos.

I can see the poets throwing "poets" into the massive chasms at
the Brow (metaphorically).

I can see the Overpoets observing this.

I can see the poets striving to be Overpoets—outstretching at
the Mountain Brows overlooking the city, believing that, with

the Verse of the Emergency Present comes not only responsibility, but even self-sacrifice.

I can see the Overpoets as easily as one can see the midnight moon, yet, at first, as difficultly as one can see the afternoon sun.

I can see the poets, now, overthrowing corrosive "poet"-editor-professors of MFA writing programs.

I can see how each writing program must be inspected by I Mortaristi disguised as writing students.

I can see how young we are and, therefore, innocent-appearing enough to apply and be accepted to these Programmes on the educational administration's assumption that we want to measurelessly learn, not scrupulously inspect.

I can see us steadfastly scrutinizing the MFA programmers everywhere!

I can see I Mortaristi envisaging the dissolution of corrosive MFA programmes, altogether, since the world could stand to lose so many of them, rather than standing to lose so many souls of poets ceaselessly sacrificed to the Molochs of Postmodern Thought and Postmodern Thought-Control!

I can see many Mortaristi, still in high school, applying to aforementioned programs, to stake them out, to infiltrate as deeply as they see fit for the cause, to disrupt any further deformation of impressible poets into anti-poets.

I can see our main act of "terror" being the raising of our hands in class!

I can see us, now, knowing: electricity is the blood of inspiration, and inspiration is the blood of electricity.

I can see us, now, cross-examining our instructors before our classes begin—testing them outside the classroom!

I can see us, now, saving the next generation of poets from "poetry"—the next generation, whose back-turn's wind will

scatter the ashes of post-modern thought across the wasteland of
humanity's collective memory.

(I refrain: In the emergency present, a poet must be willing to
live by his poems, and even die by them, or be a poetaster in the
eyes of the people, and in the eyes of the Stranger.)

I can see the Overpoets, now, compensating for the cowardice
and godlessness of the past two generations of poets.

I can see the Overpoets, now, hoarding responsibilities, filling
the Tandem-made vacuum inside of human souls—which are
nearly empty—with Atlasian loving, with wisest directions, with
vatic singing, with manic's afflatus!

I can see the Overpoets, now—onus-hoarders, over-responsible,
singers of a verse that heals!

I can see the Overpoets, now, overhearing the poets bitterly
joking about how superfluous the poet is, despite this truth: the
poet is as essential as he chooses to be!

(((O)))

I can see us, now, quitting mass media.

I can see us, now, seeing that wars generate capital, further
and further the debts of countries, demoralize the human spirit
and strengthen the central banks that we must dismantle.

I can see us, now, fathoming: the mass media distracts us
from the very things it should be revealing to us.

I can see us, now, comprehending that biblical phrase:
"Woe unto those who call good evil and evil good."

I can see us, now, knowing we must break the tableaus of our lives,
which we will truly direct, if we might un-divide and un-conquer
ourselves in time to awaken from the sleep-work of our lives.

I can see us, now, seeing to the ends of rainbows!

I can see us, now, natural, again; human, again; rightly, again; godly, again—

I can see us, now, seeing we must unknow so much of ourselves.

(((O)))

O, now, listen, know: our masters have intertwined "conspiracy theory" and "madness" like two first lovers to discourage us from taking the time to "entertain" them, and, so, too many of these cocoons of theory do not turn into butterflies of truth … Our masters convince us—through the mass media, through the education system, through the means that they own—to consider conspiracy theories synonymous with madness and foolery, so as to prevent us from discerning the conspiracies of these very masters, to make us question our own sanity if we even acknowledge *such theories for a moment. There is nothing more advantageous to conspirators than if all those they conspire against believe conspiracies do not happen.*

Flavia, Amos and Niccolo ascend the sky-blue table, where I stand.

While Flavia and Niccolo deal with a rowdy student in the crowd, Amos says: "Well-l-l, this is fun; I'm mind-blown, my man, and as you can see, I'm not the only one!" Amos not only "discovered me" but saved my life, saved my soul, preserved me in ways no one else knew how. Amos understood and understands, along with the *language* of my spirit, the dialect of my spirit's centre. I lowly sing to him:

Dare we, dare we, now, brotherly discoverer; dare our comet-keenly spirits see through the narrow needle-eye seemingly overlooking our paltry visions?

Dare we, now, dare we, mapless and guideless, see through illusions of importance, which hang like densest fogs around a Siamese light-house—dare we, then, finally voyage on feet-bottoms so untraveled they're light-speedy, charged, charged, charged enough to drive us on as, I envision, two off-white beams of our eye-lights, shooting toward that unloosening eye; illuming, suddenly, before us, a levitating bridge ... and we'll wonder: dare we, dare we cross the hovering cobblestones like beggars do a street toward a Salvation Army, on the coldest night in fifty years?

Dare we, dare we, now, brotherly recoverer of my life, lime-light-bringer-and-singer-for-moments, lime-light-blighter-and-ouster-for-moments, wisely tired of fame before the fame is won?

Dare we, now, dare we burst forth like two myriad-mile darts of light that beam toward the bulls-eye of the far-flung orbits of the Kingdom, our target?

Dare we, now, dare we, brotherly discoverer, equally equipped, ramble, march, crawl or even be carried toward a way no one goes for fear of being blinded by disillusionment, which may or may not await them?

Dare we, dare we, now, forwarding with wonder, wondering with wisdom gleaned in earlier times of our witnessing eyes, seeing to it that we know which way to trail-blaze by simply finally beginning the universal strut—charged, untraveled, mapless, but knowing the way, somehow?

Dare we, now, dare we?

"Hell yes, we will dare," Amos replies, smiling.

I can see us, now, de-programming ourselves; unbecoming the parts of ourselves infested with Tandemic evil steadfastly transmitted to us by newspaper articles, by news broadcasts, by radio shows, by televisions, by popular music, by the educational systems, by the puppet-governments. I can see us re-naturalizing, re-humanizing, re-spiritualizing.

I can see us, now, beheading Usura with the edge of our own minds and the sharpness of our own cries.

I can see us, now, knowing you can either raise and shoulder your cross on lily-whitened paths, which may lead to conflict,—but conflict that is essential to the preservation, and transformation of humanity—or you can peaceably go on, rejecting your cross for the shadowy path toward service to the Tandem; eventualizing only the deformation and degradation of humanity.

I can see us, now, seeing we DO have a choice between existing blindly in cowardly comfort or living open-eyed in courageous worry—seeing we MUST decide here, now!

I can see us, now, dreaming of this very moment, years ahead.

I can see those of us with children, now, withdrawing them from their Tandem-run schools, whose Common Core curriculum is deliberately slouching, more and more, toward meretricious demonism.

I can see us, now, comprehending the state of our nation, which is over-populating with debt-slaves.

I can see us, now, spending a surplus, owning our own bullion some day, owning our own futures, which belong to the Tandem, so long as we are in debt to them—and I know so many of us who have become not only financially indebted, but also spiritually indebted.

I can see us, now, boycotting slave-driver chain-diners, and, together, eating the food of this country—always at small-time family-owned restaurants.

I can see us, now, comprehending our breathtaking toil, realizing we are all slaves, realizing some people are only slaves because they will not free themselves …

I can see us, now, quietly acquiring gold, gold, gold; always carrying as little cash as possible.

I can see us, now, hoarding all that gold, gold, gold.

I can see us, now, shyly but assuredly contemplating guns.

I can see us, now, acquiring arms, privately owned guns.

I can see us, now, digging … burying guns, so that we may still possess them after a massive false-flag-sanctioned gun-grab commences, and the Tandem begins inspecting our homes for any possible fire arms.

I can see us, now, debtless!

I can see us, now, refusing the mark of the Beast.

I can see us, now, creating, at our collective mailbox, a catalogue of our talents and capabilities, so that we can trade them.

I can see us, now, trading, bartering, deprogramming ourselves of credit, debit, and paper currency, diminishing our tax bills.

I can see us, now, in the shadows of many laws against these proposed practices, and I SAY: FIGHT THESE LAWS, until you are, in the light of many dawns spent free in the open.

I can see us, now, together, imaginative, brain-stormy, discovering escape-plans.

I can see us, now, seeing that when the rounding ups of Beast-mark-denying dissenters commences—the rounding ups, which will conclude with deportations to the empty and awaiting FEMA camps of North America—we will need hide-outs.

I can see us, now, stealthily cultivating our own crops, speaking audaciously in soft whispers, in innovative codes, emboldening our neighbours to also do the same and thus preparing for the approaching absolute currency crash.

I can see us, now, united, eating scrupulously well, thoroughly invigorating ourselves with exercise, vitamins, and prayer.

I can see us, now, foreknowing the forthcoming Tandem-ignited Colossal Crisis.

I can see us, now, sipping Prosecco, toasting La Famiglia, since it is familial power that will be at the centre of our rebellion!

I can see us, now, fathoming that family and extended family will be our best, most enduringly loyal allies.

I can see us, now, sipping Prosecco, toasting La Famiglia.

III. *Il Mortarista: Orphomusocracy*

Wouldn't it be beauteous if an ORPHOMUSOCRACY
—a nation freely living to the rhythm of music within the hold of
inspiration; a nation consensually controlled by inspiro-electro-
musical, super-sonorous frequencies—is transitionally employed to
precipitate, and eventuate the final stage of Mortarismo … which
entails the proper proclamation, or heralding, of the Second
Coming of the Living Christ; which entails humanity's earthly
freedom; which entails humanity's Heavenly Salvation, one that
is currently unavailable to most of us, who are unwittingly
programmed to worship the Devil, as aforementioned? … Long
live the Orphomusocracy and the inspiro-electro-musical
deprogrammization of our psycho-spiritualities, and the eventual
cleansing of humanity's very souls, which, by the Devil's magic,
have disappeared from human minds.

((((O))))

Freely thinking Man, so you think only you can
have a thought on earth where verve is bursting
inside everything—you with the forces and freedom
to command a cosmos absent while you plan?!

Revere the spirit inside the insect! Man,
know each flower's a soul that faces up to our
one Mother at dawn; know all metals repress
mysteries of love; all things feel and all's in your power.

Watch out: in walls without eyes are the glances of spies.
Any matter has a verb attached;
do not use it impiously.
Hiding seraphim often dwell inside the vaguest beings.

I take some deep breaths. I take another sip of the cool spring water.

I refrain: to those of you who loathe having enemies, there is a way to rid yourselves of them all: by loving them, by approaching them with sublimely diaphanous forgiveness, by exuding, in their presence, a palpable aura of bona fide bridgeunderlust. Unless they are truly snake-spined badly people, they will no longer be your enemies. Now, the Tandemites—they are a special sort of enemy toward whom we must be aggressive, in one way or another: be it in words, in songs, in demonstrations, in Art, in rioting, in guerrilla warfare, in revolution.

A little too overcome with afflatus, I light a cigarette.

(((((O)))))

Sometimes I wonder if what our society deems "madhouses" are really the last standing Temples of God in our civilization; I wonder if many of the "insane" are satellites and mega-phones of God. Lucifer, too, has churches and satellites and megaphones on earth, but his bodies are NOT in hospitals, no. Those manipulated by Baphomet, or at least those who worship him, are out in the world and thought to be 'sane'. The richest of them are the rulers of, at the very least, the Western world. Lucifer and his "human" rulers wish to control the satellites of God, the speakers of God—so many of the "INSANE"—or at least SILENCE these who speak the truth—as fearlessly as children who have never been punished, as truly as Adam and Eve were pure before the Serpent came—for they are a threat. The newest psychotropic medications disable these satellites from properly receiving transmissions of light from the Creator. Baal, whose agenda is transmitted and eventuated by our masters, is petrified of the word of God; and some-times this pure word, this pure light of God is transmitted through certain human prisms who exist mainly in hospitals, never to be known by humanity. These imprisoned human prisms of God's essential light are meant to be refracted upon all.

There is no better way to quiet the voice of God and his true prophets than to create an apartheid between the society of the "sane," and the society of the "insane."

Now there are officers next to the guards. I take one of my cigarettes, break off the filter, then light the end with one of my final three matches.

All the world's a stage, and, in the shadow of our mass-media-synthesized struggle, The Devil dreams the future of our ongoing play. Now, know: we can continue to act out his tragic earthly play, or, break our collective human hypnosis, our collective act, and overthrow the Director and his human associate-directors. We can end this play, and begin truly living!

The crowd roars louder than ever.

(((((O)))))

*There was a time when poets lazily reflected society, like a
relaxing pond reflecting the sky. But now that humanity and
Nature are on the brink of extinction, and in need of evolutionary
redirection, and spiritual resurrection, the poet can no longer stiffly
reflect; but must rather boldly direct, the world—with wisdom,
with spirit, with mercy.*

*I refrain: The Overpoets will be charismatically oratorical,
will strike a lost chord with the masses, which poets have lost,
especially during their poetry readings—they should really be
poetry* singings.

*And as for those who do not believe in truth—they are less
likely to ever want to discover anything even remotely true, since
the quest for truth is dead to them, in their hearts and in their
minds. As a result, they will not only fail to be seekers of truth,
but fail to be speakers of truth, fail to be fighters for truth, fail to
be champions of freedom of speech; and they will be tamed and
pacified by their own fashionable nihilism; and they will never
be ones to finally discover they are asleep, and, thus, will be
beast-marked with microchips in their right hands.*

*Now mockingbirds sing strongly on the fig-bough
and O their tweets do burrow through my mind
like autumn wasps might burrow through a fruit
whose quaver in the wind might rouse them all
to sting the flesh, and core; and more than once.*

I'm faint as years-old gossamer. Niccolo and Amos rush
up on the table.

"Get yourself together," my brother whispers, "and
meanwhile I'll hold their attention; I'll tell 'em what I told

you when we smoked in the courtyard when I visited you at the hospital.

The girl in the camouflaged shirt passes up more cool spring water to me.

Niccolo booms with ardour: "In the vein of my brother's oration on Orphomusocracy, I would also like to express my love of, and address to you my thoughts about, music. I love music. To be more precise, I love classical music (and have listened almost exclusively to classical music, all my life). From age six, I have thought classical music to be the norm and have, unlike most pop-music-listeners, found pop music most difficult to listen to—likely because I have never gotten used to it. Since the birth of the culture industry, music has been qualitatively degenerating because of the standardization of popular songs. The question remains: why has the culture industry failed to ensnare me as it has the vast majority of the public? Due to my piano-playing experience, I decided, a year ago, to start writing music myself—a decision I like to think is based on my own desires. But can a person living in this kind of consumer society—where industries target potential customers and artists like prey—have desires independent from the ideologies of his/her culture? The truth: people cannot distinguish between cultural ideologies and their own desires because their desires are products of their responses to that profitable music to which they most often listen.

"In the 1800's, why did the Lied—which can be understood as the major influence on modern standardized music in that it incorporated a lyrical melody, background music, repetition and refrains etcetera—not become the standardized form for artists? Why has the Lied become standardized today, thus presenting no options in the structural form of music for consumers to choose from? Why does the music industry refrain from promoting musical forms such as a fugue, toccata, or sonata, to name a few, from the vast array of forms present in classical music? The answer is obvious: the music world has been bound to the industry's tactic of standardization, the distinguishing factor between classical and pop music. In 1944, Adorno and Horkheimer coined the term, "culture industry."

"The use of the word "industry" draws similarities between the music industry and other industries in that both manufacture vast quantities of consumer goods that are produced with the prime aim of profit-making. The Lied has been standardized because it offers a simple, formulaic structure that encourages productivity due to the relative ease with which a song-writer can complete a piece. If everyone were writing fugues, it might take an artist decades to produce one album.

"From a young age, I noticed the standardization of music; I noticed a strict formula the majority of popular songs followed. I soon realized the differences between the music of modern bands are trivial, almost unnoticeable, and musicians are mainly distinguished from one another by image and appearance. Image and appearance have become standardized as well. A term worth mentioning is "pseudo individuality," which refers to the idea that "the culture industry's assembled products that have made claims to 'originality' ... exhibit little more than superficial differences." I fully agree with Adorno and Horkheimer because I have felt the monotonous effect pop music can have on the brain as a result of the variety-lacks. I noticed as a child that songs, in general, exhibited: the same time signature, 4/4 common time, as though it were the only time signature to guide a song; the use of simple rhyming patterns; a limitation in the range of melody to no more than an octave and a half; the same harmonic chord progressions (for example, I-IV-V-I and the chorus being rooted in V); the excessive use of repetition and refrains (a common structure being: intro, verse 1, chorus, verse 2, chorus, bridge/guitar solo, chorus, end).

"The key question is: how does the standardized sound of today's music attract consumers? Why do people embrace this standardized sound? The music industry, by nature, maximizes its profits by selling products designed with a pre-given formula that ensures consumers will be attracted to it, which is no different than the way McDonald's incorporates a strict formula of calculated ingredients, developed by experts, to ensure that the experience of eating their food is as desirable and addictive as smoking. Standards in music are created as a result of the process of competition, whereby established standards are imitated, and therefore, become frozen. These standards have a pre-calculated effect that the industry uses to make more profit. For example, the endings of songs today are usually their beginnings, and act as a summary of the song to help listeners remember what they have heard, to reinforce the main theme of—"

A beat.

"The police are going to have my brother apprehended!" Niccolo exclaims.

I hear boos and yawps and caws of the song-drunk crowd.

A gang in blue approaches my soapbox.

"Crito, please come down from the table," a policeman demands firmly yet respectfully.

"We've gotten nearly 100 complaints about your raving from within a one-mile radius of the campus," another officer states.

"They're going to arrest him against his will because of the unique state of his mind!" cries a student.

Niccolo, Flavia and Amos ascend the table again.

"We're gonna have a riot on our hands, you magician, you!" exclaims Amos, amid the proto-palpable fervour in the air.

Niccolo looks stressed and exhausted, yet he raises my hand in the air like a boxing ref might raise the hand of a victor.

"Salute!" exclaims Amos.

"Kabooooooom!" Flavia blasts, while the wave of boos and rage and ovation rocks us.

A wide, long chain of nearby students spreads between the table whereon I stand and the officers preparing to apprehend me.

"Officers! You're clearly violating Crito's democratic right of Free Speech," cries a student.

I am being apprehended under Section 17 of the Mental Health Act. *Please allow the officers to do what they must.*

The crowd grows in belligerence. Some students go toe to toe with the officers.

The officers break through the wall of students.

I co-operate peaceably, encouraging students to make way and shy down.

By the time I reach the cop car I realize I have left, in my wake, a riot.

Flav, can you hand these pamphlets out to the students for me, after things settle?

Flavia nods. Since I am cuffed, she searches my bag and finds a bundle of three-paged pamphlets, containing the following:

Page 1. PHONETOVERSE

Terrace Sonnet (Dove + Cardinal + Hawk)

In Memory of Doria Di Carra

Cheer, cheer-cheer, cheer-cheer;
wha-cheer, wha-cheer, cheer-
cheer, cheer-cheer. Coo-ah
coooo, coo-coooo; coo-ah

coooo, coo-oooo. Wha-cheer
wha-cheerooweeroo-
weerooweercheeroo
coo coooo. Wha-cheer, wha-

cheer, cheer-cheer, cheer-cheer
coo-ah coooowha-cheer
wha-cheer wha —*KEEEEEEEEER!*

Coo-ah coooo, coo-coooo
Coo-ah coo-ah coooo;
Coo-ah coooo, coo coooo

Page 2. VERSO D'OGGETTI/OBJECTVERSE

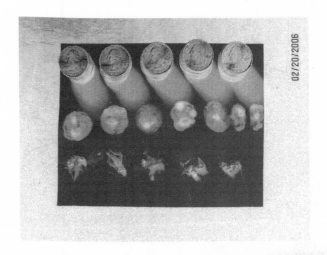

Here is objectverse—in this case, objecthaiku, a form I invented while in my early teens. In this exercise, and possible art, of verso d'oggetti, each object equals a syllable of haiku, and so there are 17 stationed things. In verso d'oggetti, things can easily rhyme, or possess rhythm, in density, shape, colour, substance etcetera ... Dark, dense, heavy objects may slow rhythm down, like stressed words. A line of coke may quicken a line, since each white speck looks the same as the next, and arguably creates quicker mental ingestibility. Bottle caps can quasi-rime with quarters, and a lego block might quasi rhyme with a sugar cube etcetera.

This is primarily an exercise for those poets who have lived so long in their heads, or in their ivory towers, that they have literally lost touch with the things of this world. From Left to Right (coin-stacks + human blood smears + dead crickets). Note: crickets bought dead.

Page 3. Objectverse (out-take)

Marc Di Saverio

"You made me realize the mirage of my own being today," a student reverently yells through the back window of the police car wherein I sit, awaiting my trip to the Hamilton Mountain, to the Sanatorium ...

Through the cold, gray cage, just before he drives away, I exclaim to the officer:

And they shall call for the implantations of microchips in our right hands!

And I proclaim this microchip is verily the mark of the Beast!

And now you know but, still, will you take the mark of the Beast?!

And you won't enter Heaven if you take the mark of the Beast!
I pause.

... And what if we created a Musocracy, a society ruled by Muses/Inspiration (I have already invented an Inspiration-Generator!); or an Orphocracy, a society ruled by Music. Or how about a synthesis of the two: an Orphomuscocracy, a society ruled by Inspiration and Music, which *would transition humanity toward its possible—if not spiritual—physical salvation!*

The cop does not respond.

I realize I must truly cool down now, for the sake of my health and for the sake of the revolution.

In a gentle yet firm whisper I sweetly sing to the officer:

I knew a lonely vagabond who swore,
up and down as my Sisyphusian
perpetuity, that a poltergeist
beat his heart, that he gave his soul to Baal
at eighteen—not for some wobbly stardom,
not for Baal's hand to guide his fingers on

his first guitar—for his little sister's
liberty since, one daybreak, during her
first week of high-school, Sylvia was
snap-fastly possessed by Baal while high
on her swing in the family yard. Following
weeks of priests, of howls, of baritonic
screamly laughter, of levitations, of
sudden cuts, of threats; her older brother,
the lonely vagabond I knew, desperate,
gave his soul to Baal in exchange
for Baal's retreat from her green-blue body
and infiltration into his own. I met him
in the cliff-facing courtyard of a psych-
ward, as I did a second vagabond,
who cast out Baal from the first and into
a vulture—whose whereabouts are unknown,
whom we witnessed flown against the wind,
breaking his gyre—toward lightning-sheets,
toward thunderclouds, breaking his gyre.

VIII. In the Skin of Three Patients

Poems composed at St. Joseph's Hospital after my apprehension at McMaster University.

I. *The Paralytic*

The voice that through the iPhone orders false-flags,
orders half-masts, orders mourning through its
broadcasts, that raises questions why is always
silenced; and I've been blind from phosphorus ever since

the dawn-raid outside Raqqa, where my youth,
like a ghost, lags behind the young but never
haunts these lasting few—in rags, still rambling through
red rubble. The ears that through the radio

hear the false words, hear the drummer-boy,
hear the screaming of the rocket's drive; that hear
the secrets of the mighty, never hear
the roar of battle—and if, if only I

had known of voices through the iPhones calling
false-flags, I wouldn't be calling for the nurse
—the nurse whose body's ways I'll never know—
to put me into bed! to put me into bed!

II. *Une Chanson D'Amour D'Un Esthète Cyclothmique*

A   *(the glass ideal)*

And her vermillion hair,
curved along her forehead like the blade of an ancient sword,
                    quavered.
    Fearless, beaming, free,
                I had silenced the soiree.
I waltzed among the mannequins
        then loafed upon my fire-flowering soul
                on the dance-floor.

… She goes by Joan—a poet, studying English at U of T,
        writing a thesis on T.S.E.
We smoke some Camels with the campy kids on the balcony.
    And her vermillion hair,
as though Boccioni-sculpted, dynamized her Galatean face.
Joan said she's the heiress of
        Friscolanti funeral homes;
that her twin sister's dying of
        Hepatitis,
                and her parents don't care.
    And her vermillion hair,
                a tableau of my esprit,
steered me when she turned her head …

B

The aesthete—as picky with his mates as the poet is with his
     words—would rather die alone
in the arms of a statue of
Galatea the Beauty
than in the arms of
the merely pretty.
And her vermillion hair,
sixth-sensed, mirrored me my mania with sheen ...

And her vermillion hair
     has been glueless from the rain—
and now I understand the Kinks' *All Day And All Of The Night*.
And now and at the hour of crickets' play
     the first gray cloud
     turns gray-gold.

C   *(a sonnet of two juke-box selectors)*

with Joan, at the Inter Steer Tavern

https://www.youtube.com/watch?v=usNsCeOV4GM
https://www.youtube.com/watch?v=b97hqSDRspw
https://www.youtube.com/watch?v=1w7OgIMMRc4
https://www.youtube.com/watch?v=PbgKEjNBHqM
https://www.youtube.com/watch?v=b8-tXG8KrWs
https://www.youtube.com/watch?v=_l09H-3zzgA

https://www.youtube.com/watch?v=S-Xm7s9eGxU

https://www.youtube.com/watch?v=IArfrd14scw
https://www.youtube.com/watch?v=Pu94mWlgzMY
https://www.dailymotion.com/video/x1xu5f
https://www.youtube.com/watch?v=E9rNLnLyutM
https://www.youtube.com/watch?v=zdmAN_xSJKw
https://www.youtube.com/watch?v=0U_jGVEKr9s

https://www.youtube.com/watch?v=6OFHXmiZP38

D

No Quarter blasts the campy Pomos out
into the offshoot street, and all the while I
yawp and howl behind the turn-tables—new
Technics—and link my arms with teetering
friends whose mouths now sonic bloom
the first verse of the *Ocean,* then cease
when Joan comes in like a late wan
ray through the eye of a boy
sprinting to make his first curfew—
bloodied by the bullies who pursue him
like autumn wasps on a garbage day.
Joan yells over the waves of people,
but like Marcello on the shore in *La
Dolce Vita,* I cannot hear the voice,
only waves. And her viridian hair,
damp with fierce tears and first rain.
I don't care anymore, she decompresses
with a stare that glares black gleams
of distance and dolour I too share in loving her.
The solar days of flavouring the air
with dare-traced auras are over, and the days
of stuffing pillows into basement windows
have just begun. Joan, in my arms, cries *No!
No! I'm snuffing it!* Joan, my cousin Jason
and I unite our souls of single dots
connecting into a Bermuda Triangle
for Joan's arising and propelling thoughts
of cliff-jumping into her twin's embrace.

And now I wonder if she will ever
chase a dandelio-clock again, if
she will ever dye her hair vermillion,
or dance to robin-songs in the dawn of
spring, or start a riot from her bed. Last call.
Showers beat upon the bar's front door
like a manic in a bubble-room. Crying
before me, Joan knows I know she knows I
know she'll snuff herself and I can't save her—
Joan, you really must be hospitalized!

E

These backward-flowing tears the nearest breaking
but withheld, soak my spirit in purest ablution,
grieve the Almighty unto a new waking,

turn murk to shine in my third eye staking,
drown my treading urges to disown.
These backward-flowing tears the nearest breaking

but withheld from bursting in her eyes' reflection,
oasis my mind with the tears she'd have undone,
grieve the Almighty unto a new waking.

I sit on her chest so she can't try to run
toward the end of her greatening aching;
these backward-flowing tears the nearest breaking

but withheld, sear my exit-impulse snaking
through me like sewage through a snow-stream,
grieve the Almighty unto a new waking.

My eyes reflect her pale, razor-shaking,
wrist-ward fists I pin like poison moths, again.
These backward-flowing tears the nearest breaking
grieve the Almighty unto a new waking.

F *Hokku*

11:11 under the moon—
while I make my wish,
my wish comes true.

G   *Aubade*

I wake to wha-cheers from her windowsill.

A breeze of flower-blends enters her room;
her upside-down blue roses do not sway.
The skyline seems like our conductor's wand;
her house of get-well cards still stands today.

Like wind shakes dew from a bowing petal,
the Real shakes my dream of being her groom.
Upon my sweat-beads flower-blends now settle
with the waning scent of her new perfume.

Arising, I hear her bath water flow
—is this what Keats once felt for Fanny Brawne?—
Arising, I open my eyes to the dawn:
why are my socks all wet and red and cold?

Like an old man's map of the world I fold.

III. *Serena's Voice*

No more will I endure the nightly measure
of my own father's guiltiest pleasure.
I'll beat his lie-detector-cheating esprit.
My mood, up and down as Sisyphus,

never escapes the spectrum of depression
nor reaches kinship with the risen sun
nor finds a space where I can madly fuss
to anyone, even myself, can cuss

aloud, feel warmth from your embraces—none
of which I remember, like an old actress done
with feeling kisses on the stages. And thus
I hold an empty needle and a gun—

the shining knight now comes to oust my pains!
One. Two—goodbye my slithering veins,
good-bye O loves my heart could never know,
my birthdays when you'd ride down hills of snow.

Good-bye, you man-handler who made me
a pan-handler; Good-bye, mother—and you world
who saw me degenerate, yet called me daft
when I accused—when you, like Icarus, just laughed.

IX. Il Mortarista 2

I. *Plasmadians*

Could it be that it's an invisible
yet detectable electricity
connecting the dots of the stars of the Universe,
keeping the suns and the planets in their places?
Could electricity, that filamentous
force, out-matter gravity?!
Amos, amid the twilight, lightly tip-
toes glowingly toward me, as though
striding a tight-rope of my eldest dreams.
Niccolo, Flavia, Amos
and Laura (the girl with the camouflaged shirt),
as well as three hundred others are here—
ones who saw me blasting on the sky-blue
table-top, with hand on hip, wherefrom
I was descended and apprehended,
wherefrom, contra my conatus, my
illumining spirit was divided from
the darkening ones, then contained
inside the super-tinted police cruiser
like a virus inside a laboratory—
wherefrom, in the wake of high rioting,
it dragged, like a funereal opera,
toward St Joseph's, for a 'quieting,'
with shots of Haldol—inside the bubble room—
and lots of Clozapine, each juxtaforced

into my bloom of soul whose pollen of glow
thus may be low in the dying twilight now.
And Flav, Amos and Niccolo waited till
the right's councillor showed, and signed
my discharge form before me faster than a master
forger pens a promissory note
before some sun-blind teller at the bank—
after which I coma-strode out
into the open evening. I swallow
three days' doses of my angel-
upper—Dextroamphetamine—that I
might break the sleep-knot of the downers,
that I might re-engage with those who stood
both amid—and also then withstood
my blasts of afflatus in that sand-brown square—
who now top the ancient cliff, whose north-
faced waterfall's loosening stones
glimmer vermillion. The cricket-music
rises with the yellowing fires
flickering up into the fireflies,
into the brightening constellations.
No back-turn's wind will sweep the shardy stars,
No Agency will waste Nature's nurse.
No Iron Hand will bend these bars of verse.
Some will come in the name of the LORD and proclaim:
"my miracles are really in His name,"
yet, in fact, they will be of the Serpent.
Beware of those who come in the name of the Christ
and, as I continue to thrive in my
Christian-hood, in my vision-hood, beware
of even me. Behold my imperfections;

behold my package of Marlboro Reds,
yet, too, behold the bar I overleapt—
the bar that trussed me from asphyxiation.
And behold this "madman," or whatever
I am, always apprehended when
about to blossom into tuneful timelessness;
when about to arm-wrestle the media-
cast, massive invisible hand that's pricked
our wriggling kind upon the stinging
pin of its faithlessness. Beware
of those who come in the name of the Christ,
blazoning to be The Glowing Ones.
Behold my imperfections—especially if
you see me perfecting—even if I seem
to perfect myself as fast as loose November leaves
blow from trees in massive blasts of wind.
Jesus Christ is perfect in every way.

Behold Amos; behold the Torch of the Sublime,
which he has steadfastly sustained above
the miasmal waters of postmodernity,
all the while treading the nauseating
sea, or treading the stony sea-floor—
slowly, forwardly till, finally
reaching the shore of the future, where we
now stand. O, what on this earth, and what
in that Heaven, would I be, if not for
saint-bold Amos! Behold, I'll be terse
as time's few guarantees; behold the widely
galaxies, the universe amid
the skies, and the universe amid

these words, which may be akin—as stars
are akin to fireflies—to the universe
beyond the skies. I'll be terse if you will
simply behold the electrical universe.
O, what on this earth, and what in that Heaven, would I
be, if it were not for Amos Heine!
And maybe even the tumour-enormous Einstein
will be foot-stooled by this "madman"
or his mentor tonight, as you will all,
—there, and there—hear the news that stays
news. And, tonight, let's hold each other tightly,
thereby holding onto to-mor-row-w-w-w, singing:
La la, la la la, la la la la la la la la la la
La la, la la la, la la la la la la la la la la
La la, la la la, la la la la la la la la la la
La la, la la la, la la la la la la la la la la …

Amos raises his voice: "Bless you, Crito! …
I do not know whom or what in Heavens
this Crito Di Volta—a-singing here—IS;
I do not know whom or what in Heavens
this Crito Di Volta—a-singing here,
a-beaming here, a-loving here—IS;
and Crito himself does not know whom
or what he is, do you, Crito?" I do
not respond, but dragoon a spacious smile.
"Crito, are you holding fast to some big
secret?" asks a blond, almond-eyed
pregnant girl. *If I do* hold
a secret, I do not know *the secret.*
I'm a forevermore unfolding answer,

just like all of you! "Crito?" Amos asks,
"will you now sing the electrical universe?"
My ebbing heart begins to rise again,
then, forthwith, I feel like a freak-show …
Why don't you introduce yourselves to me,
just as you would not introduce yourselves
to a clairvoyant monkey at a carnival?
"Well, Laura—" Amos begins.
Besides Laura, I end. I lower
my head. *I lower my head,* not *because*
I'm super harrowed, but because I un-
remembered: a messenger need not meet
those he reaches. Dammit. I've behaved
so infantinely. I raise my head:
please forgive—I pray, forgive—
my fit, I atone, then kneel on
the graffitied, jagged rocks and loosened
stones of the Flatrock grounds. There is silence
save for the bonfire crackling on Scenic
Drive. "There is nothing to forgive!"
Flavia out-cries, then, continues:
"Viva Di Volta! Viva Di Volta,
who emboldens and illumines us all—
I know it, and I think they all do too!"
Then, everyone spontaneously stands
to ovate—O—me; I withhold
weighty tears while I, too, arise
to my feet. "I'm Vincent Weston," cries
the poet who incited me, "and I'm
Renton Daniels," cries the professor
who ridiculed me. *Crito Di*

Volta. I nod to both of them, my eyes
browsing from eyes to eyes, from soul-
windows to soul-windows, around which crowd
the snow flurry-soft faces of
silent children, who peer inquisitively,
receptively. O Amos, Il
miglior Fabbro, I think to myself.
O Amos, Il miglior Fabbro, I boom.
Flavia descends the Flatrock with
Bruno Grunn, a university fop,
while the others cheer for Amos. I yawp.

II. *Dreams in C Sharp Minor*

O, now, listen, know—this is my hypothesis on electro-magnetic fields, which invisibly live. Someone hissing in the dark, through what seems a mega-phone, bursts into the bonfire light. Bruno Grunn. But why? And where is Flavia? Ahh, Flav is trailing him. She approaches. "Crito, I tried to avert him from exposing aspects of autumn 2015." *Flav, I do* not *care if* anything, at all, *about me, is revealed, since I wish to be diaphanous. Please, stop worrying!* It's true. I do not fear Bruno Grunn will hit his target of my heart, which beats to the will of, and by the massaging hands of, the Living God —nor do I fear he will stake-burn my cred as Generation Zugzwang's horizon-riser. "I am come to unveil what I believe is key for all to know about Crito, who, in one day, has established and expressed phenomenal thoughts and feelings, has won out hearts, but beware of this, this ideologue?—This prophet? This fool?—and longingly look into his alien past, I wish to relate his Facebook post from October 15th, 2015."Amos breaks forth like lightning, then issues a hauntingly beauteous moan of protectiveness. *You may read whatever you like,* I reply as lovingly as I can. I irrelevantly think to myself: 'I need to stop listening to Rock n' Roll music, that extraordinary McMusic, of and for the Beast! I irrelevantly feel ease in the truth that I mean to do what is right; if I fail them, I am faithful in their forgiveness, because I feel their love for me will be bona fide, as is my love for them, reciprocal as first lovers who elope and marry and remain as faithful to each other as they are grateful for each other ... I must trust my own—vital?—words, which seem, more and more, to be transmissions from The Stranger, and not thoughts from my own mind. "That fall, he posted this on F.B. This is, by the way, public information that no one has really discussed openly, at a place like this, where there might be scrutiny, since we need to ensure we do not endorse an extensively psychotic and perhaps dangerous —at least in theory—rebel, like Crito. I come to light the way of another tunnel of his essence, and to assure that we are safe in his unprecedented presence. Don't we all just want a safe space? No matter what?" My stomach turns like a skipping record. "I digress. Here is what the poet and painter Facebook-posted on the aforesaid date (I *am* Facebook friends with Crito, by the way):

"Family, Doria, Friends, e Tutti: Inside this eerie bedlam by the bluffs—you could clean this place with all its tears—I fight to fathom who I am: My mother was born on Christmas Day, my father on the summer solstice. My brother was born on Easter Day, and I on my parents' anniversary. My father's name, numerically, equals 137; my mother's name, numerically, equals 137. I was raised on San Francisco Avenue, in the San Neighbourhood—near the West Mountain Brow—where the streets are named after saints. The *33* Sanatorium bus still winds throughout these streets—one may hear it from my childhood home, whose number is 1101.

"Throughout my life, numberless people have testified that I have either saved their souls, saved their minds, or saved their corporeal lives.

"In my boyhood, I endured a connective tissue disorder that ensured the onset of Pectus Excavatum, which means the mal-forming of cartilages, near my sternum; and eventuated the grotesque caving in of my chest, by 13, when my gasping deepened with every passing day—I gradationally asphyxiating. The hideousness of my body excruciated my mind, dashed my self-image, spent my self-worth, to the point that my nickname in high school was the "mute," for, I almost never spoke. For 9 years I did not sincerely smile, dragging myself like a half-blind cab-horse, too old to be drawing anything but air.

"At 21, I underwent the Nuss Procedure, an experimental operation—to possibly truss the excavatum into convexity. A one-foot-long, one-inch-thick, bowed steel bar, was forced through my right side, then inside my pulmonary cavity, converting asphyxiation to easy breathing, concavity to convexity, disfiguration to beauty. After a week of recovering I was released from the hospital, on my birthday; in myriad ways I was still 13. The Nuss Procedure left a 3-inch-scar, where my right side was penetrated. The scar still very visibly exists.

"In the summer of 2010, I heard what identified itself as the Voice of the Father of the three-Personned God. He said I would be henceforth transmuting into a secret being, whose identity I too, alas, would not know until absolute transfiguration. His sublimely vivacious voice disclosed that I'd soon be in the hospital healing patients, that seraphim would shield me from demons, that I'd soon be, as I should be, freely sermonizing to the patients, and that I'd never have to depress about corporeal repercussions for voicing the Truth, for voicing His Vision. Soon after, my family hospitalized me because I had been insisting I had been directly corresponding with God.

"One mid-summer morning, after having sermonized for an hour, I finally sang the coda of the Voice's transmission through me and toward the patients. We stood beneath a red-roofed smoking pavilion, which sheltered us from the elements—it had been down-pouring from tenebrous clouds for an hour and a half, amid the steady, seemingly inexhaustible lightning that was striking everywhere, like riled yellow vipers—waiting for the wind-whipped rain to cease so we could return to our respective wards (we were on 'passes,' as they are called). Startlingly, two demoniacs, in blurs of wide spasmodic movements hyper-generated by the notable force of the Devil, burst upon us. Both youths raged rabidly; both riving the restless crowd, screaming immeasurably discordant baritones; both asserting their Latin petrifyingly precisely; both, at last, settling, upon the long pavilion picnic table. I forthwith shot toward the two youths, each foaming and seizing till apparently exhausted from the merciless exertion perpetuated by the power of the Devil himself. I firmly, but calmly lay my left hand on the one youth's head, and my right hand on the other. *O Satan, in the name of Jesus Christ, the Saviour of us all, and the Son of the Living God, flee from these two boys at once! Flee from these two boys at once! Flee from these two boys at once!* I tore my crucifix from my neck, then, with the force of the Holy Spirit inside me, pressed it into each of their chests, imprinting it over their hearts. Just then, two shower-weary mountain vultures, alighted a nearby statue of some lobotomising doctor from the early 20th Century. At once, I cast, like two eternally long shadows, both demons, into the mountain vultures, which up-circled into a gyre that soon broke into zigzagging over the cliff, when, overtaken by a whirlwind of rain, the gyre reunited in a dance puppeteered by greatening gales, till both mountain vultures were, at last, steeply flown into the cliff-top, both impacting simultaneously, both lingering in their lives, their necks and bones as blasted and shattered as humankind. The two youths lay exhaustedly unconscious on the picnic table. The lightning was striking everywhere around the pavilion, steadfastly, even striking the stone body of the lobotomising doctor. The lampposts were so tipped that I felt like I was in some early German expressionist movie, and saplings were uprooted within heavenward whirlwinds that dropped them back to the earth, after the winds stopped whirling. And, alas, the patients were ripped about, one to unconsciousness. "Make it stop!" screamed a wind-shoved woman in white. Then, forthwith, driven by the Holy Spirit, I leapt out into the gales and the rain and the lightning, then raised my arms, like a ladder, into the disorderedly pouring sky. *O Lord who stands on air in Heaven, hearing this prayer, O put to death this pitiless storm!* Over the next moments, the lightning lessened, the gales turned to winds and the winds turned to breezes. Within 3 minutes the colossal storm ended. Some of the patients panted, while others sprinted from the pavilion to the Sanatorium doors. Just as staggered as they, I shadowed the door-ward patients swiftly striding ahead for what took about thirty seconds, after which I found myself dry as the others. Only light rain resumed, very soon after our dash back to the Sanatorium doors. Soon, it was rumoured that I had dried a downpour, pulled down the winds, reversed the lightning.

"The next day, some patients accosted me, inquiring if I might heal their minds of their illnesses, if I might lay my hands upon their heads. They had come to believe I possessed powers, or lived as a channel—a vessel—of the Lord, his mercy, and His words. *I will,* I evenly stated, since I then remembered what the Voice had said before my hospital admission. I lay my hands upon their heads … Many said they were healed; I was especially effectual in exorcism, and at healing the depressives and the drug addicts. Some said they believed themselves healed, but only when my hands were upon them. More and more patients approached me with vehement wishes for healings. I was released, re-admitted, released, re-admitted, eventually seeing I needed to disremember the plausible miracles behind me, along with deep wonderments about my identity, all of which exhausted the high spirit inside me. In a world where soulfulness is scrubbed from people like mildew, so miracles are absurd-seeming to all.

"On Holy Thursday Evening, 2014, after having wept for the Christ—I had been especially envisioning Judas' betrayal, Jesus' arrest—I had whimperingly watched all of Zeffirelli's *Jesus of Nazareth*. I prayed to The Lord: *I do not know who or what I am. Can you please tell me who or what I am? Can you please give me a clear sign, even though my transfiguration is incomplete?* After praying, I fell asleep … I awoke, on Good Friday Morning, with an extreme, unimaginably piercing pain in my right side, in the very place where I still have the scar from the radical NUSS procedure. The stabbing throb in my right side was so overcoming that I yelped and screamed out to my family, amid miserable throes. A seraphim visited me in unexplainable, electro-magnetic vibrations, stressing that the stigmata in my side would immediately begin to divinely fade, then completely disappear by Monday Morning, at which time the piercing in my side completely ceased. Yours, Crito."

The fire rises up into the night. Amos throws Ashbery's *Self-portrait in a Convex Mirror* into the bonfire.

"Well what have you to say about it," beckons Bruno Grunn.

I do not *have anything to say, yet I do* not *have anything to hide. As far as any one should be concerned, I am Crito.*

III. *La La, La La La …*

Could it be that it's an invisible
yet detectable electricity
connecting the dots of the stars of the Universe,
keeping the suns and the planets in their places?
Could electricity, that filamentous
force, out-matter gravity?!

I afflatically sing into overdrive:

The moonish half-light of science has
eclipsed the suns of mythology; and the keys
to astrophysics, to nanophysics,
to the gears of existence, are bundled
inside ELECTRICITY. I believe,
with Velikovsky, that myths of yore now jangle
these keys; that the incredible events, both natural
and, to our minds, supernatural,
the tales of above and below depicted in ancient
myths cannot be accounted for as mere
aberrations of the psyche, as Jung
would have it, or of historical subterfuge,
as Graves would have it. No! Let's credit the gifts
of our ancient ancestors! They told, as we
tell, what they perceived with their keen senses!
Dismissing what another has witnessed is
stealing another's heart, dishonouring his mind,
denigrating his life! We must not stoop so low,
must only stoop to come down from the plinth

of our self-congratulation, only
to ply our imaginations to the rich
realms in which others have suffered and thrived
and recorded their riveting lives! These
strange-to-us phenomena, in ancestral
skies, can only be explained by ELECTRICITY,
by her sister MAGNETISM, and by her
sister LIGHT; by the careful, plodding paths,
the dead ends, the incremental advances of
observation under the dun and un-
spectacular aegis of natural
philosophy—the true physics?! Even today,
as I speak, steadfast intelligences
reveal how electrical discharges, created in
laboratories, appear exactly
as cave-paintings all over the world.
Take, for instance, the Wheel of Emanation—
call it plasma; call it quantum fluid,
the Higgs field or what you will; for,
ETHER has many names. This wheel
is its mark and seal, which reveals itself,
both large and small, above and below, by
microscope and telescope, in magnet
as in Nebula—for what is the snake
that devours its tail on every continent?
And what the cosmic column pin-wheeling
the low ancient sun? And also, in every
continent thus: I have Amos to
thank, for opening the 'eyes of my eyes.'
Amos bows with his orange-yellow torch—

the crowd explodes into more ovations.
It was during a vision near Armageddon,
when Amos, a soldier of the Israeli army,
realized his callings as Seer,
cosmologist, and poet. He returned
to Montreal, his birth-place, penning
and lecturing on numerous subjects
—especially verse and cosmology.
His father, Avi, died when Amos was
a teenager and so the great mentors
of that language-enraged city, helped raise
dew-diaphanous Amos, teaching him
to read music and compose in heroic
pentameter. With the enshrining of
falsehoods, and among the flimsy paper
generations teeming and organising
into ever-greater corporations,
with the Age of Giants at hand, Amos
picked away at the wallpapers of
mendacity to reveal the dry rot;
and he dedicated his lives-like life
to the revival of vital ETHER —
the lost, most essential element,
which lies at the heart of creation; the
ZERO at the crux of the Cartesian
Plane; the origin and sum of all measures.
To this principle and to the Holy
Spirit, as much as to Verse, he dedicated
himself, jangling by my raving ear
the keys to our deepest questions that, by my

raving mouth, I might impart like a host
of flaming arrows or a many-tongued
lightening bolt to YOU, my loving listeners.
I hand out self-drawn pictures of plasma:

Here is what plasma discharge looks like under a microscope and
this is what a Nebula, in deep space, looks like! Many cultures
around the world employ different myths and paintings to
portray the same cosmological phenomenon. Then there's the
image of the four rivers radiating from the centre of the wheel of
the sky, to the boundary of the wheel:

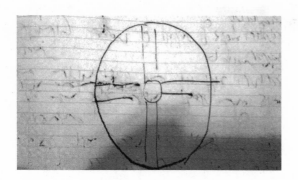

Could it be that, by a forensic approach, we can truly fathom the meaning of those most flabbergasting ancient myths?

Laura winds down the Cliffside toward the guardrail. I fast-draw a cigarette from my breast pocket. As I strike my match, a massive gang in zombie masks sucker-bludgeons the audience with hammers, sucker-stabs the audience with neon knives, jump-kicking and jump-punching into the petrified crowd. Amos chokeholds an assailer off his feet, then, after slamming him into the denticulate ground, *refuses to* release his grip on the masked-man's throat. *Amos!* I cry. Amos presses his thumbs into the ski-mask sockets, screaming. He releases his grip in time to roundhouse into another masked man about to strike me in the back of the head with his green Easton bat. The thug jumps up and jabs Amos twice in the face—only enraging Amos, who foot-sweeps him into the fire. Amos and I go back to back, now, as one unit, then bloody and uppercut a few more of them, after having taken some monster blows ourselves. As I catch my breath, I see Flavia and Niccolo back to back—one unit—staving off two more assailers with zombie-masks, one of whom Flavia upper cuts from behind, in the back of the testicles. Niccolo—his nose now bleeding—apprehends another in an arm-bar, breaking the assailer's appendage in two places. Niccolo hasn't been in many fights, but he is a natural fighter! Amos smiles at me from across the way. As he shoots toward us, one of the masked men throws a pale of gas or paint-thinner upon the visionary. *No-o-o-o-o!* I scream. "Amos!" Niccolo warns. Equidistant to Amos, another assailer creeps forth with Amos' torch. I sprint forth and tackle the man, just before he can reach Amos. I jab him twice then flying uppercut him into the flames. *Amos! Run from the fire! Run into the bushes, bros! Run!* Amos dashes deep into the forest on foot-soles of near-silence, barely shaking the bushes. Finally, the assailers sprint down the Flatrock and onto the trail leading to Scenic Avenue. Some of us, still standing, push forth in pursuit; yet we soon see that we have no chance of catching up to our attackers. We stop, turn, then retrace our forward steps back toward the Flatrock to tend to the wounded.

IV.

from: Amos Heine <the.montreal.prize@gmail.com>

to: Crito Di Volta <patient.power@gmail.com>

C

... I'm still in the bushes ... My advice: don't orate for a
decent while ... Lay low, network underground. Those were
no vandals, but hired hands of the Tandem. Meet me at
Hortons in 45 min.

A

X. A Second Letter to Flavia Vamorri

from: | *Crito Di Volta <il.mortarista@gmial.com>* |

to: | *Flavia Vamorri <bakuninite.2000@gmail.com>* |

Happy twentieth birthday, Flavia!
I painted you a portrait of L.G.!
I'll bring the piece to the Brow, tomorrow.
You can add it to your Liam knick-knacks.

Hugs,

Crito

XI. A Visitation

I.

Thirteen days ago, while celebrating twenty years, Flav chalked
    yays for the first time, proximately prompting in herself a
    further episode of mania.
While periodically peering over my shoulders, I fast-step
    Fennell Avenue toward Saint Joseph's Mountain Site,
    holding blue orchids inside a clay vase and glimpsing the
    Starry Shuttle, which has never woven wild silk—
    constellation of the Bull, with lasso round the throat,
    unable to pull its cart; the million stars of the String-Net
    so well-made for hares it cannot catch; the Fan which
    never winnows; the Spoon that never measures oil.
And the worldly kind of craftsmen accuse the Celestials of
    imposture, incompetence. This poet states: *They're*
    radiant! ...
While passing through the Sanatorium doorway like a master
    sewer's thread through the eye of a needle, I realize:
    revolving doors would fit this place the most.
I wonder: has Flav been Seroquelled, again, tonight?
Her Icarusian mind has blown skyward like a bright red leaf
    about to land in the gutter of a ghost-street.
Her Icarusian mind has blown skyward by the winds of
    mania and here, there, breezes of her falling-fears—she
    must always be rising to feel just right.
And her mind—sometimes—holds two; so, now and then, I
    arise with her.

Her Icarusian mind: a phoenix falling to calmly waters
    outside the Samos Isle.
Her Icarusian mind: a phoenix rising through raining rays
    above the Samos Isle ...

I knock, moonlight-lightly.
I revolve the knob softly—slowly—then gently swing the
    door to Flavia's room, so as not to wake her from her
    "sleep," as one nurse called it ...
    and O!
    O!
    O!
I dart forth like a flaming arrow speeding toward an assassin
    about to slay a new Queen already beloved by the poor
    and the lowly.
I execute the tackle just right, but bang my head on window-bars—
    And O the ... spinning floor ...
    And O, I see triple ...
    and O ... I ...
awaken unto a lesser dizziness, tipping this way and that.
Flavia, Seroquelled into immobility, was—was being sexually
    assaulted in front of my eyes, by the R.N., *Raymond Hedley!*
And Flav is sans her usual understanding of matters before I
    can really begin to understand them.
"So *you* think the others'll believe you over *me*?!" laughs
    Raymond Hedley. "I'll just say I foxtrotted into this
    room, doing rounds, and surprised you amid sexually
    assaulting a poor, catatonic Flavia. And *so* many of the
    staff already think that you are *super* into her."
My finger-nail-driven palms now know the burning
    locomotion of the blood inside my forearms.

Before I can lash forth, he pivots, dancer-like, drawing a Swiss
army knife.

As he lunges forth with blade in fist, I jab him in his lightless
eye with my dove-white fountain pen. The Cross's blue
ink runs together with Raymond's blue blood.
Pamela, Flavia's nurse, enters the room, upon hearing Raymond's
searing screams; my pen planted deeply in his face like the
pole of a standard in some newly-won soil.
She answers Flavia's moans with a distant yet somehow
warmly embrace.

II.

Raymond's screams of rueful wonderment and self-
lamentation—not of any atonement—unnerve Pamela.
Raymond finally strains my pen from his dead right eye,
then promptly faints: from shock or blood loss. "What the
hell happened here?!" Flavia whispers: "While I lay prostrate
from the Seroquel, still *awake,* still *aware*—look, if it were
not for Crito's visit, Raymond Hedley would have raped me."
Flavia eschews her eager tears. Soon, all at once somehow, a
wave of vivacity blossoms her pupils and crimsons her pallor.

III.

After relating our testimonies to some soullessly inquisitive officers, Flav and I prepare to leave for the hallway. I upraise a foggy Flavia, who founders into my arms, with which I carry her out of her room. I search for a chair, but do not find one; so we sit on the floor, both still shocked. Flavia leans against me, our backs to the north wall, our legs out before us like stopped clock-arms. 'The psych ward's narrow hall of howls is very long but not eternal,' I think to myself, not knowing why. "My will to electrify the Patient's Rev is hella stronger, now, Crito, since, I have not only witnessed this reprobate System, I have now quite suffered and survived it. Thank God for this shock I feel, which will, I hope, immunize me from PTSD," Flavia discombobulates. "I must affix on and delight in the numbness of shock, I guess—I must wretchedly revel in the inner glade between my self and what has happened." *Hedley-y-y-y-y!* I lament. An officer inside of Flavia's room nods to us as Pamela points and points at us with nuances that hint: 'Crito and Flavia carry some worth, but they are still sub-humans—Crito and Flavia carry some worth, but they are unequal to the sane. Flavia continues: "the dictatorship of the psychiatric patient will be achieved even sooner now. The System will be dismantled and rebuilt: from within *and* without. There will be both predetermined and spontaneous uprisings at St Joe's, and there will be simultaneous intifadas co-ordinated inside the world's most prominent institutions. The worldwide Rev will begin in all three worlds at the same moment! Then, the Rev will naturally circulate to other sanatoriums like pollen does, in a vigorous wind, to neighbouring towns. All insurgents will be tied by their wills to the Rev., to one common list of demands; refrained, again and again, by ambassadors of the Revolution. And, in these aforementioned, simultaneous, pre-plotted intifadas, guerrilla patients will take fellow guerrilla patients hostage, consensually, of course. Both hostage and hostage-taker will shadow each other into dual self-defence from our enemy. And, the revolutionaries, from Port-au-Prince to Toronto, will be disciplined to shoot our enemies—security guards, soldiers, officers—below the waist." I press record on my iPhone for the sake of historicity. "My cugino, Armando —a made guy who lives in Palermo, will arm our rebels, and, likely, will agree to advance us, in solidarity, whatever we need—cause, see, he's been hospitalized, uncountable times, for Schizophrenia. He can fathom our marginalization." *Hey Flav*—"do *not* interrupt my thin stream of consciousness, which is all I have dividing me from an army of trauma." *I'm so sorry, Flav.* 'She seems different,' I think to myself, not knowing why. "I cannot wait to detonate the bubble rooms. I cannot wait to kidnap the assaulters in the System. Our list of demands will include: swift implementation of this law— to receive a psychiatry licence a doctor must score over eighty percent on an emotional intelligence test; food breakthroughs; mass handovers of reparative capital *and* criminal workers of the administration, whether their rank is high or low; the definitive discharges of select patients, such as political prisoners; the inversion of the smoking policy; re-distribution of psychiatric power, via the Vortex Accords you initiated last summer; the passing of the executive orders composed the time we bussed to Montreal; and more and more and more and more and more. So long as my list of demands can wrap my soul's wide wound, like a bandage, the doorway to forwardness seems somewhat possible. I'll not, like a mummy, lie petrified inside the tomb of my basement bedroom. If even a few of the uprisings succeed, the world would suddenly know the patients' powers, now wouldn't they? Who the fuck would ever fuck with us, again, if we executed what I've just proposed? Who would still suppose the so-called insane are wholly powerless? We will *take* our equality, which is the only way we will truly receive it, and, the world—even the blasted, double-edged mass media— will finally see that we will no longer be abused, raped, used by our own "caretakers," shamed, despite being the ones who steer humanity. While the populace doctors other sorts of minorities with speech sensitivity, the language tied to those who suffer severe, psychotic disorders, continues to colour our conversational speech. People cherry-pick which terms to be mindful of, not knowing, or not caring, about the message they are transmitting to those excluded from their progressive dialogue, which makes others like us, with psychotic disorders, feel subhuman." My instinct to oppose her will to language policing is fully eclipsed by my instinct to allow her thin stream of consciousness to flow freely. "For those whose own minds are often hellish places for them, having others—even strangers they overhear—declare to them, through their word choice, that the condition of this minority does not warrant the same sensitivity as all the others, is dehumanizing. Why the fuck are there no safe spaces for the brothers and sisters society deems insane?! Why?!" Flavia bangs her fists into the floor. "Why should society care?! Why should society care!? Because the relation between madness and creativity is no longer only founded on art serving as an outlet for suffering. There is a fine line between madness and genius since, recently, as if society would care, scientists have proven that the two share a similar genetic makeup, called Neuregulin 1. We revere and adore van Gogh, Woolf, Plath, Cobain, Sexton, Nash, Nelligan, Hemingway, and other great minds affected by mood disorders, or schizophrenia; we love our mad genius, we are eager to take his gifts, but we most often reject the very illness that spawns the gift, and thereby reject the person. Those who possess the combined traits of creativity and psychiatric instability, and can harness their aptitudes and channel them successfully, are the fortunate ones—those able to make, of their horror, something essential to the world. However, these very same geniuses could, under different circumstances, be the homeless individuals—in the streets and passage-ways—from whom the people veer away, or at whom the people whisperingly jeer on the bus, as the geniuses grapple with often untreatable psychotic symptoms." A beat. I continue to record Flavia's star reflecting stream-of-consciousness; I look into her dilated eyes, seeing her essential place in the universe. I approach the nurse's station. *Do you have an extra chair so that Flavia can sit?* One of the male nurses coldly hands me a steel chair. I turn around to see Flavia fighting tears upon the brown ground … I slowly help her up. Flavia braces herself. *Oopalla—I hate to see you cry, but maybe it's best you just let it out, rather than hold it in, you know, Flav?* "Fuck letting it out! Fuck my own Passion, Crito," Flavia belts, her face quaverlessly clear of tears, which she has withheld. I see a million-man march of the mad!" Flavia exclaims. "And I'll recruit guerrilla-patients from the many online psych ward whisper networks. And I'll recruit my friends from Mad Pride, who know it is impossible to be proud of one's self when one is not only openly treated unequally, but one is also scorned, mocked, hated, abused, mistrusted, beaten, murdered … Flavia cuddles my hand. Pamela reminds, "I know this is an emotional time, but you know the policy on patients touching, or getting too close, which is unhealthy. You know the rules." Flavia jolts, her mind seemingly struck by sheet-lightning of afflatus, which is better than her mind being struck by the vipers of her traumas. Again, she shakes her fogginess. With her lips against the phone, Flavia continues: not only will the psych world be faced with our revolution, so will anyone outside the system, who treats us sub humanly, who thinks we are not worth as much as so-called sane people—and that means a WHOLE LOT OF MOTHER FUCKING PEOPLE— and they will answer to us. The news of rapes, assaults, degradations, and other forms of ill treatment occurring herein, NEVER reaches the minds of the masses. More and more underground mental health activists are turning to Revolutionaries; it is our time, Crito," she declares, taking my hand in hers again. "I'll seek out like-minded patients. O Patients, we must lash out of the closets, lest too many of us die by our own world-guided hand, or explode upon the world that jeers us! Like, who really cares for the rights and lives of the patients? How many souls are paling downtown in the streets tonight, in the alleys, in the alcoves; poor, dilapidated, 'vile bodies' … And now, with intifada's force, at last, at last, at last, our 'ship of fools' docks at the Bay of Honour and Equality; at last, at last, at last, our 'ship of fools,' with revolving 'crazies' as its captains, barges into the large and empty yachts of the fogless harbour; and crashes into the shore of the world that has exiled us … at last, at last, at last, the rocking of the boat now ends and, for the first time, we stand—stably—upon the sturdy earth." *This will be our Santa Clara! This hospital will soon be ours! A guerrilla unit of eighty patients! The world will know the patients' powers!* I sing; how could I not? "Viva la revolución de los pacientes!" Flavia yawps, so the whole ward can hear. *Viva-a-a-a-a!* I bellow. Pamela scolds us with a glower as she hears us from inside Flavia's room. "Viva la revolución de los pacientes!" Flavia yawps, so the whole ward can hear. *Viva-a-a-a-a!* I bellow.

XII. La Strada

I.

Under the storm clouds and topping
the snow hills, Flav and I
finally see Tristan Dion,
dragging his death-wound-deep buggy

behind him …While withholding his cries,
Flav and I embrace him
at once, his ID circlet still

around his wrist like the dimming ring
of some undiscovered planet.
March is the month of the homeless's

hope, of first warm rains,
of first warm winds rippling
inklings of the truth inside
them: Spring *IS* near!

II.

"Why'd you run away from the hosp.? And then from your mom?" Flavia asks, while I pass Tristan a just-lit cigarette.

"I ain't goin' back to that hospital, ever," begins Tristan. "Listen, I'll *tell* you why I ran away from the hospital and from my mom: in the 'System,' you're only treated as well as you're loved. Those who are cared for on the outside of the Sanatorium are also cared for on the inside of the Sanatorium—their loved ones on the outside make sure that they are treated well. Those who are not really cared about on the outside, well, they are not really cared about on the inside—there are no loved ones on the outside to ensure their good treatment. Crazies, like me, are seen as sub human, since it's clear we aren't naturally worthy of human love—at least, the crazies without families. I don't think humanity has very much love for our kind."

Tristan adjusts his black eye-patch.

"Flav, I'm stuck between the lovelessness of the hospital, and a mother who does not love me. Wouldn't *you* run away from both of 'em if you were me?!"

Flavia looks away from Tristan for a moment, then returns her eye contact: "I hate to say this, but I can't answer your question, Tristan. All I know is that Crito and I love you *bottomlessly*; we want you to stay with us for as long as the winter continues to be so wintry, you know? You can stay with us; one night at Crito's, one night at my place?"

We enter Jackson Square for some warmth. Tristan lets go of his buggy.

XIII. Times with Tristan Dion

I.

The nights that Tristan Dion stays with me,
we work on En Masse Deprogramming;
now that he's a Mortarista, too, we'll
further reverse the speed, then further speed

the reverse of humankind's pre-plotted
slide-away. Through the nights that Tristan
Dion stays with Flav, they prep the Patients'
Rev. He's *Flav's* comrade, too—(and lover, maybe?)

Let us go out back into the shed,
where Triss and I set up, like suns, the first
En Masse Deprogrammers, which reverse
one's psycho-spiritual rot from

over-exposure to evil concentrate
via mass media, via other means
aforementioned ... Behold: three Mortaristi
–all Zedders or late Millennials–

sitting, head-phoned, before MacBook
Airs; while I count them down from ten to one,
that each might undergo Deprogramming—
a process wherein one unlearns what I

Mortaristi deem must be unlearned
–History, as it has been told by its victors,
for instance—at the speed of light. So
far, eighty per cent success rate! *Three … two …*

II.

    While Tristan Dion singingly perfects his heavenly fade,
my eyes—inside the mirror of my room—fix upon his
eye-patch. He bursts into a smile, inside the mirror, like a
white rose might burst outside a window.
    "So, what do you think of your new cut?"
    I adore it, brother. Maybe you should become a barber?
    "Nah. My real love is boxing."
    Really, eh? You never told me that.
    "I could never go pro because of my eye."
    Ah, man, sorry to hear that.
    "Yeah, me too; right now, I'm about Tyson's age when he
won the heavy-weight championship from Trevor Berbick.
    I exhale.
    "This is one of the best cuts I've ever gotten, Trissy."
    "Listen, Crito, I was thinking—as you know, I *am* a
doubtless believer in Christ—do you think … you could give
me vision in my right eye? I believe in you, Crito—"
    I arise from the makeshift barber chair.
    Sit in the chair.
    Tristan promptly obeys my gentle order.

I remove his patch. I softly place my right hand upon the naked cadaverous lid of his blind right eye. *O Jesus of Nazareth, O the Redeemer, please heal Tristan of his blindness!*

I remove my right hand from Tristan's right eye, whose tears flow down my wrist.

Tristan shivers in the mirror, while I stand stock-still.

Open your eyes and, for the first time, see the world through both.

Tristan's thin, spasmodic eyelids slowly, flutteringly open.

"O, O, I can see through both my eyes! By the Lord in the Heavens, I can see through my right eye! Crito! Crito! I can see your tears with both my eyes, I can see your eyes with both my eyes, I can see your whitening soul with both my eyes ... And, O, I can see my future with both my eyes!"

As Tristan arises from the chair, his quaking legs give way; he falls to the ground with his eyes still blinkless since their opening.

Are you afraid to blink your eyes, Triss? Do you fear, in a blink, your sight will disappear? BELIEVE! O, BELIEVE! Believe in Lord Jesus.

While turning toward me he finally blinks his eyes a few times.

"Yes-s-s-s-s-s-s-s!" he explodes. "O yeah-h-h-h-h-h! I can still see through my right eye!"

Tristan turns back toward the mirror, and, for the first time, looks himself in the eyes.

I kneel.

XIV. Enter Sergeant Ivan Proschenko

I.

Tristan, Flavia, Ivan and I, either by illness or by subterfuge, entrenched the psych hosp. cliff-topped on the Hamilton Mountain, one month back, insuring the germination and bloom of the Patients' Revolution, whose first operation— twenty-five synchronized attempted coups throughout the first, second and third worlds, "from Port-au-Prince to Toronto," as Flavia has put it and as Flavia has planned it—will, according to Ivan Proschenko's estimation, triumph, "in at least twenty percent of insurgent Sanatoriums."

II.

Ivan fought in the war in Afghanistan for five years and, after his tour, spent five years in the PTSD Unit. After hearing of our revolution, he rallied other veteran patients to the cause—many of them disillusioned with the health care system/Big Pharma and, too often, with humanity itself. Other veterans here, for the first time in years, feel they have a new raison d'être—to liberate other vets and other civilians, who are being denigrated, abused, sub-humanized, raped and mocked by those of the very system that should be uplifting, soothing, humanizing, and aiding them. The four of us, the "generals," stand beneath the smoking-pavilion. "Between twenty-five and seventy-five revolutionaries reside in each of the other twenty-five sanatoriums around the world!" Flavia exclaims. We yoked *eighty-two* insurgents—more than any other set of generals collecting recruits for the Revolution sprawling all Three Worlds of the earth—because of Flavia's ardently breathtaking, automatic speeches. The worldwide uprisings—three days away—will dawn at this very hour. I've decided, despite my rank, to be the drummer-boy too, with blessings from the other generals. This is not to say I will not be armed, will not be fighting, will not be leading.

XV. I Break a Pact With You, Ezra Pound

I break a pact with you, Ezra Pound—
I have protected you long enough.
It's time for me to make new friends.
Like lightning from a snow-cloud

you shocked the Lost then lit their way,
and struck all sorts of mortmain;
sublimely impossible, you realized
everyone's dream, yet, *were* your errors all

extensions of magnanimity?
I break a pact with you, Ezra Pound.
You *know* I never cared for the occult;

you *know* I never cared for your hate.
We share some blood but not one soul—
let there be difference between us.

XVI. A Translation of "Canto I" from Dante's *Inferno*

When midway through the journey of our life
I found myself within a dimly wood,
where the straight way I'd been walking was lost,
and O how hard it is for me to speak
of just how stubborn and savage this rough wood
was, the very thought of which renews my
fright, this wood just slightly sweeter than death,
but to tell you of the good I found therein
I'll firstly speak of other things I saw.
I cannot even rightly say just how
I originally entered that place
and I was so exhausted by this time,
when I deserted the way of the truth, yet,
when I reached the foot of a hill, where the valley
that had pierced my heart with fear, came to an
end, I looked up and saw its shoulder brightened
by beams of that sun which leads men right, on
every road; then the fear that had settled
in the lake of my heart, through the night I'd
spent so miserably, becalmed as a panting
man, escaped from deep seas to the shore, who
turns back toward the treacherous waters
and stares—so my fugitive mind turned back
to see, again, the pass that no living
human ever left. After I rested
my body a while, I made my way again,
over barren land that's always bearing

upwards to the right; and behold, almost
at the start of the slope, a lean fast
leopard with spotted coat, which would not turn
from before my face, and so obstructed
my path, that I often changed back, so I
could retreat. It was now early morning
and the sun was mounting up with myriad
stars that were with him when heavenly love
first moved all delightful things. That hour
of day, in that sweet season, gave me fair
hopes of the bright-coated creature, but not
so fair that I'd avoid fear at the sight
of a lion that appeared and seemed to come at me
with raised head and rabid hunger—so that
it seemed the air itself was afraid—and a she-
wolf seeming full of craving in her leanness
and who had, before now, made many men
live sadly … She who brought me such heaviness
of fear, from the aspect of her face, that I
lost all hope of ascending; and, as one
who's gain-eager, weeps, and is afflicted
in his thoughts if the moment arrives where
he loses, so that creature, without rest,
made me like him; and coming at me, bit
by bit, drove me back where the sun is silent.
While I was returning to the lowlands,
one appeared, before my eyes, seeming hoarse
from some long silence and, when I cried
out to him, "Have mercy on me, whoever's
there, whether actual man or shadow,"
He replied to me: "not a man but once

a man, and my parents were from Lombardy,
from their native city, Mantuans.
I was born Sub Julio, though late,
and lived in Rome, under good Augustus,
in the age of false and cunning gods, and I
was a poet who sang of Aeneas,
that righteous son of Anchises, who came
from Troy where illustrious Ilium
burned, but you, why do you turn your back
on such sorrow? Why do you not climb
the beauteous mountain, which is the birth
and cause of all bliss?" I meekly replied:
"are you Virgil, then, that fountain-head
that springs so great a river of speech?
O, light and glory to other poets,
may that lengthy study—and that vastly
Love, that made me scan your verse—be worth some-
thing, now, for, you are my master and my
Author, and you alone are the one from
Whom I learned the lofty style that's brought me
laurels. See the creature from which I turned back,
O Sage, famous for wisdom, save me from
her, she who makes my pulse and veins quaver."
When Virgil saw me weeping, he said to me:
"You must go another road if you
wish to escape this dismal place, for this
creature who so distresses you allows
no man to cross her path, but instead obstructs him
to destroy him, and has so vicious
and perverse a nature that she never sates
her ravenous appetite—and after she eats

she's even hungrier than she was before!
Many are the creatures with which she mates,
and there will be many more until the Grey-
Hound comes and makes her die in pain. He will
not feed himself on land or wealth, but on
wisdom, love and virtue, and his birth-place
will be between Feltro and Feltro, and he
will be the redeemer of that lower
Italy, for which the virgin Camilla
died of her wounds; and Euryalus, Turnus,
Nisus and he will chase the she-wolf
through every city until he has brought
her back to Hell, from which envy first loosed her.
It's best, as I think and understand, for
you to follow me, and I will be your
guide, and lead you from here through an endless
space where you will hear the desperate hollers,
will see the ancient spirits in sorrow
so that each cries out for a second death,
and then you'll see others at peace inside
flames, because they hope to come, whenever it
may be, among the blessed. If you
wish to climb them, there will be a spirit
fitter than I to guide you, and I will
leave you with her when we part, since the Lord
who rules above does not wish for me
to enter this City, for I once fought
His law. He is the Lord everywhere,
but there He rules, and there is this city
and his high throne: O, happy is he who
chooses to go there!" And I said to him:

"Poet, I beg you, by the Lord you
did not acknowledge, lead me toward where
you said, that I might escape this evil
—or worse—and see the Gate of Saint Peter,
and those you make to be saddened." And then
he moved; and then I moved behind him.

XVII. Fuse

Although the Patients' Rev. is nigh to dawn upon
humankind, I am drawn to dream of the future of I Mortaristi.
Whereas the Patients' Rev., made for a minority, works best
theoretically; the Mortarist revolution, made for everyone,
works best in practice.

Experiencing de-institutionalization, I'm seeing again the
struggles of the everyman and the everywoman, whom I miss,
really. I feel I'm meant to be a voice, not only for the very ill,
but for all humankind—which is not to say that I am no
longer a comrade of the Patients but, rather, that I wish to
share my life and vision with everyone.

XVIII. Jump Cuts

I.

Requiring a titanic diversion from our forthcoming uprising and, simultaneously, requiring funds for the sexually assaulted patients of St Joseph's Hospital (its directors refuse to compensate any of them), we brainstormed, then finally founded the Festival of the Silenced, which is scheduled for this Saturday (on weekends there is less security at the Mountain Site).

A few months ago, in Toronto, Flavia met Josh Homme —the singer for the Queens of the Age—backstage, at one of their shows. Homme, awe-struck and inspired by Flavia, and Flavia, impressed by the brilliant and accomplished star, bonded strongly, and she became his muse. They have met more than once, and have been texting, video calling and writing each other since the night they met when Flavia, a natural-born singer, so breath-took the band with her own rendition of "Little Sister" that they asked her to accompany them on tour as a backing vocalist, but Flavia declined because she needed to be near the hospital to treat her condition. Besides, even going on tour with a rich and famous rock band and making lots of money would not distract her from her true calling. After the Queens of the Stone Age agreed to play at the festival, Homme invited Pete Townshend—a sexual abuse survivor—to perform with Roger Daltrey as The Who. Additionally, my brother—and I am most happy about this part—will be playing 7 of his classical compositions for piano, accompanied by a Mortaristic light show I've developed to heighten the depth and transcendence of the Niccolo Di Volta experience. My Bloody Valentine's Belinda Butcher will be performing solo, Tristan Psionic will be reuniting for the Festival, and more …

II.

Facing the edge of the Hamilton Mountain, way past the cherry-trees next to Saint Joe's, Flav, Ivan, Tristan and I stand backstage at the Festival of the Silenced, where numberless patients—on passes—and non-patients alike, dance, sing, mosh and mingle as though at the end of the apartheid no one cares to discuss.

"I can't believe we're one hour away," Flavia sings, dancing like a seraphim would dance to Saint Cecile's latest piece.

Flavia waits for three thirty-three as a mother might wait for her first child's delivery.

III.

"Okay, shhh," Flavia cuts in, "Josh is about to sing 'Little Sister'." I agree that we should hush. "Little Sister" *is* very popular, after all, among so many psychiatric patients I know—as are so many Nirvana songs. Though "Little Sister" *is* my favourite song by the Queens, I must say I have

never been a fan of the song's coda, which I rewrote with
Niccolo after first adding an extra chorus. But I see past this
imperfection since, verily, the lyrics of Little Sister are some
of the most Romantic I have ever heard—"Little Sister" is
the Romeo and Juliet balcony scene of Rock n' Roll music,
at least among so many in the Sanatorium, where breathes
the least among the humankind in the humankind's godless
eyes. I digress. I light a cigarette. I'm already wearing the
drum-kit that Amos gave to me. Flavia excuses me while
I reach toward my drumsticks, which are tucked inside a
black Venetian satchel (bulging slightly with the pistols
my Nonno bequeathed to me).

IV. *Amico Infinito*

Ryan Milligan, a knightly rightly Mortarista, raised on San
    Remo Drive, strides toward me in the distance …
He's blasé on the Patient's Rev. or should I say, *so* engrossed
    with Mortarismo, that every thing save for his family and
    save for the Lord is secondary now, because he sees the
    Emergency Present facing his sons, facing his daughters.
We mastermind on Messenger.
We both delivered addresses in the same alley, under gulls,
    at the Rally of the Clarion Calls, but not yet vis-à-vis.
Through childhood, I'd see him on the Saint Teresa of Avila
    playground, or on the Donici dance floor, but I was shy
    and he was older, so I regarded him from afar.

Ryan is a matchless fighter; he could have gone pro, but rather,
    History-majored at McMaster U;
after his degree, he plunged into his research on military
    strategy and, soon, innovated warfare-ways he'd later
    adapt and apply online—on Twitter, on Facebook, on
    Instagram, etcetera.
Ryan trained Flavia with his most à propos online and offline
    stratagems, some to be applied today, beginning at three
    thirty-three.
His blue-gray eyes, bolder than Arthur Rimbaud's, peer
    through the face of Billy Duffy—the guitarist of the
    Cult—circa 1985, only more reproachful.
A commander, on the one hand, and a colossally popular
    fixture of the Movement, on the other; He's always
    gleaning teeming new recruits, with his irrefutable
    discourse and his irresistible essence.
An object glimmers before my eyes, while Ryan draws his
    hand from his satchel, transiently blinding me upon this
    Hamilton hill, much like *L'Étranger*'s Meursault, blinded
    on the Algerian beach.
O my God, is that *what I* think *it is?* I ask him after regaining
    my vision.
"It is indeed what you think it is."
In a recent online exchange, Ryan depicted his Great Uncle
    Conor who audaciously fought for the I.R.A. Conor
    was not only famous for his gunmanship, but also for
    his hand-to-hand, his preferred form of combat, and
    he'd often lead a charge with this six-inch blue-gray
    switch-blade, which Ryan now hands to me.

V.

It's 3:23 pm.

While Niccolo and I stand backstage together, he twice looks over his shoulders, then pulls a revolver from his jacket.

What the fuck are you doing with that, bros?!

"I'm coming with you guys. I'm in on the Rev."

O no! No! No!

"O yes! Yes! Yes!" My baby brother's smile widens to my conceding eyes.

He has every reason to want in on the Rev. I know it, and he knows I know it. He has seen what this system has done to me, and to him and our parents, in the process.

You do realize that the Rev. begins in 8 minutes, right?

"Of course!"

I'm about to ask him how he knows about the Rev., but I do not. After many years of feeling like his younger brother, despite being older than him, in this moment I feel like the elder—like in the days before I was institutionalized, when Niccolo could truly look up to me ...

We begin sprinting toward the hospital as we hear a single starter's pistol-shot, which Flavia pre-arranged with one of the revolutionaries, so that all the guerrillas would know when the first phase of the Revolution had begun. We cover our ears during subsequent explosions, two inside "solitary rooms," two inside the auditorium, where lobotomies are performed before audiences of medical students. Two bombs failed to detonate inside the head security sector.

I wish Amos were with me. Yesterday he gave me his blessings, and his strappable drum-kit, likely more out of love than approval.

I drum and sing "No Quarter" while we wildly rush toward the flaming Sanatorium.

XIX. The Battle on the Bridge and the Trials at Century Hall

I.

For, O, five minutes, now, Flav's
been holding fast her pistol to my temple,
winningly convincing the enemy that
I am a hostage, not a guerrilla.
While we, at last, outdistance the westward
corner, she unleashes me, that I might
yoke and lash at the battle on the bridge. Twelve
of the twenty-five worldwide strikes
have triumphed so far, thus spoke
the whisper-network, which Flavia avidly
made for this mission. I draw my pistol
while singing *they choose the path where no one goes!,*
drumming so hard I bust another stick;
while Flavia, through a tight, tapering,
twilit hall with a high, sky-lighted, baby
blue ceiling, aims down the zigzagging in-
door bridge between Century Hall
and Century Manor. She spins her pistols
perfectly, entrancing me a moment,
then fires toward the legs of two onrushing
officers, who seethe and scream while reaching
for their Sauers. *Dart Right!* I exclaim,
while firing at our enemies. We all
dart right like eyes across the notes of a staff—

we, mutineers, together as one music,
rolling near-right while time-bombs burst far left,
before the oncoming enemies, comprising
soldiers from the Armoury—many with
diaphanous shields, many with eyes rolled,
many with conceited expressions, many
with chins aloft, many pressing forth,
many diving down ... And, yet again, we
roll right; again, then again, and again, and again;
until, finally, we're charging toward
the venerable Century Manor,
a mansion now condemned which was
the original Sanatorium,
padlocked since the 1980's, yet still
remains a heritage site. Flav
and I rave "No Quarter"—we can not get
enough of that song, what better
song to attune our spirits to conflict!?
Outside in the twilight, Flavia
improvises fittingly heavenly
harmonies on the spot. To us, music
has become a bona fide guerrilla
force to either confuse or demoralize
the enemy, or to generally
communicate. We set toward
the east, indoor Courtyard, where
the trials of our kidnapped will very
soon begin—nurses, doctors, directors
and others who have execrably

mistreated the patients. The able-
bodied opposition retreats … "What do
you have to say for yourselves," Flavia
exacts from the two shot-up cops.
"Thank you for mercifully shooting us
in the legs?" one of the officers
replies. Flavia smiles. "Do any
of you have a cigarette," the second
officer humanly inquires. I
give the second officer a smoke.
"Whoa. Winstons, huh? Strong, huh? Thank you, son."
I tear off my shirt and tend to his wounds.
I request a drag from the cigarette.
I return the cigarette to the officer, then blow
three smoke-rings that hang loosely over
the heads of the wounded officers. "Those
are focking killer smoke-rings! Holy,"
bursts the first cop. I begin drumming
the aperture of "Baba O'Riley".
Out here in the fields, I descant. "I fight
for my meals," descants the second cop.
"Peace out," Flavia states,
while we depart to storm the Gymnasium, which
must be taken if we are to make the Trials.
We are awaited, so messages
the whisper network. "I'm gonna take a peek
on the Gymnasium," Tristan whispers.

II.

Flavia cradles comrade Tristan, who is already breathless.
"You're gonna make it!" Flavia screeches, beating Dion's
breast with her heavy hammer-fists, while I, feeling soul-
slides of my times with Tristan domino inside me,
hear three near pops. Tristan, with lead shot in his right eye,
is dead in the other.

III.

Like blood through a cut we break through the smoke
of the North Wall's detonations—I'm
howling while drumming off-beat to throw
off opposing standards inside the massive
gymnasium, where moonlight floods
the sky-lighted ceiling arcing highly
over the evening combat. We're firing
at the knees of our enemies while
four of our comrades, shot through their hearts, gasp
last words, as breathing officers down
curse our mothers. I shoot two cops
in their knees, then another in the rear.
I holster my gun so I can drum, once
more, for morale. Ivan, always
opposing the shoot-below-the-waist code,
head-shoots, indiscriminately, striking
two in the face, and one in the throat.

"I did that for morale! I did that for
morale! Now we are truly equals!" cries Ivan.
"Nonsense!" Flavia screams, three inches from
his face. While I strive to divide them,
the cops throw smoke and gas bombs toward
us, which blind me till I blink toward new
sight. I draw the grey-blue switchblade
from Ryan Milligan. I'm bulletless,
and the ammo boxes are unreachable.
I rally what remains of our platoons
then lead the charge with fiery, harmonized
roars behind me. We're ready for hand-to-hand.
Right before the standards' clash, sparks
fly from my chest. I lie on the wood of
the gymnasium floor, hearing curses—
the grind and squeal of the machinery
of war. Flav and Niccolo are by my side,
with faces funereally emptying
through their blackening shock.
I feel an adrenaline jolt; I arise
with my eyes still closed, then hear a near-
synchronized gasp. I open my eyes.
A near cease-fire ensues, as many gawk,
ooh, and jaw-drop; shocked, I stand
with bullets in the left side of my chest,
conveniently bullet-proofed by the
solid steel truss inside me.
Before the enemies can shake off their
shock, I lead a *second* charge in this battle
for the Bridge, with my switchblade—
the rally-cries of my comrades behind me.

We—a wallop of glory, a blossom of
wrathful compassion, charge! The last
of the adversaries retreat from the Gym,
away from the Courtyard. Flavia
accosts me with a long, red-hot sliver
of steel she must have pulled from one of the fires.
Do it. She presses the steel into my wounds,
cauterizing the holes inside my chest.
I do not yelp or scream, but would have, indeed,
if it had been anyone other than Flavia
treating me … We wave to friends
awaiting us outside the Century Hall.

IV.

"Flavia Vamorri, by unanimous vote, will soon preside as
judge of this court."

Psych ward-lifers make up the jury. We voted against
court marshalling; but, instead, for fair and open due
process. Defense and Prosecution await the call for session.
A massive throng of patients—some victims of the accused—
stands before the court that slowly evolves toward its first
trial. Flavia approaches the jurors, while many warriors tend
to their wounds, drinking cool spring water, half-collapsed
on the courtyard steps.

Will you boys and girls be awake for the Trials?
"Easy for you to ask, Mister Amphetamine," Ivan scorns.
"I'll be at the Trials," assures Niccolo.

They all agree to attend. It's 9:55 pm. A breeze of flower-blends descends the courtyard, while two cardinals, despite the darkness, wha-cheer through the night.

V.

Due to a conflict of interest, Ivan has replaced Flavia for this, the third trial.

"We the jury find Jonathan Leslie," acquitted one month ago, after another mistrial linked to entrapment-charges, "not guilty."

As the judge prepares to speak, Chelsea's Father, Peter, penetrates our security, and tearfully charges toward Doctor Leslie with a revolver in his hand. As Flavia strives to tackle Mr. Swan, he fires two shots through Leslie's throat and cheek. Leslie, blood-choked and blood-ebbing, tries to murmur something, but he is as inaudible and voiceless as all the girls he has destroyed. The Swans were invited to the Leslie Trial, Flavia's long-time aim having been to give the family some closure, hoping the jury would find Doctor Leslie guilty. Alas.

XX. The Battle for Century Manor

My brother breathes then breaks into melodies
of all the major keys, blasting his pistols in
full charge against the standard opposing,
leading through the no-man's land like one
with nothing to lose, despite being one
with everything to lose, behind whom
our spirit-soaring forces drive, behind whom
I drum and rave, toward his spirit's sails,
the winds of faith I wholly have in him.
O my baby bros! Who uppercuts
two cops in one blow! Yet,
amid this electrical victory,
I hear Ezra's grievous voice: "And then
went down to the ship," a few feet away,
yet Ezra Pound's not standing there.
"Set keel to breakers, forth on the godly sea;"
I chase his voice toward the cliff-top's forest-
edge—"And we set up mast and sail on
that swart ship, bore sheep aboard her,
and our bodies also heavy with weeping"—
then, as I enter the forest "and winds
from sternward bore us out onward," Ezra roars,
blaring the cardinals out of their trees
while a red-robed man stands suddenly before me—
holy! Holy! Holy! Holy! Dante
Alighieri! Dante Alighieri,
haloed here before me in this wood
no longer dimly with the dying light!

O visage with the strangest smile!
O blackened brow and tan from hell!
O eyes wherein white sight still swims with style—
who'll out-see your eyes no eyes can tell!
I've never forgotten your diamonding soul,
away from fiends who want their victim's fate,
upon the peak where you guard Heaven's gate,
where you found peace from this black hole.
O Alighieri, guardian of grave-
yards, the array of the works you have signed with your verve
will never be wiped from the rising wall of time.
You will live as much as God Himself
since Heaven has learned, as well as hell,
to stammer your Cantos, O poet, my angel.
"Holy! Holy! Holy! Holy! Crito
Di Volta! Crito Di Volta,
found amid this wood upon a cliff,
overlooking the city he was born in.
O Crito—you sorrowed forth
like Leopardi—I love you; and, after
following my footfalls a while, you will
freely shepherd hosts of souls to Paradise,
while on your own way there—you'll understand,
like your first language, more about
just who and what you are." My whole face,
yellow from Dante's high-beaming halo, smiles.
"I'm always watching you from Heaven's gate,
which I still guard throughout sublimely days;
and, throughout so many nights, I descend
to where you are on downcast earth,
where I have stood before you, stood behind

you, stood beside you, since your birth.
I was with you those times when you prayed for a sign.
I was with you those times when you yearned for your death.
I was with you the time when you owned the stigmata,
saw what you saw and felt what you felt, see
what you see and feel what you feel, my god-
son, who as I have known you, at last, knows
me. O you, assigned to me by the Father,
before your parents ever shared a kiss.
Yet I am also here to ask you this:
why did you tie the world-bell's rope
of Mortarismo with the hyper-striking
viper of the Patients' Revolution, which
will rive the "sane" and the "insane" even more,
sowing hate in the "insane" and shame in
the "sane," naturally; and, soon enough,
unnaturally, by the Baphometians who
will shanghai, then ill-rule the Movement
altogether, whether you are bought or not.
There is one to come who's greater than you,
who'll sever the snake from the rope of the bell,
which *will* be rung—but not by you, my godson.
You will *never* ring the bell, nor hear it while you trail-
blaze your immolative life on earth;
yet, with mirth, will hear it from Paradise.
Though all of your verses were destined to be
sung, not all you say and do is thoroughly right,
for you have not wholly surrendered yourself
to the Trinity. Your entirety you'll
soon surrender, lest divinest ties are
riven asunder. Crito, follow me."

We tread some jutting stones toward a pool
where I can barely hear my leader speak
because of the western waterfall's crashing.
From the water's edge I see a near-blinding
light at the bottom of the pool, which
arises; and, O, the haloed head of a girl
shatters the pool-surface, breaking and beaming
into the air, wearing dove-white medieval armour.
Her short dark hair is cut straight across her golden
brow. She slowly steps toward the stony
shore, where I stand with Saint Dante, open-
mouthed—Joan of Arc approaching like
a Season, her endless eyes' violet beams
illuming faces of the cliff-side. She takes my
hands like highest compliments, her equatorial
ardour full-exuding from her armour—
(Saint Joan of Arc! Saint Joan of Arc!)
She pulls me toward the pool she purifies white
with her lightly multi-laser sword—the pool
of the waterfall, edged at the Mountain Brow, all
misty in the midnight, where she lays her
hands upon my head and plunges me deep
into the water with the vehemence of
a teen suppressing, into her subconscious,
some unattainable dream for which she can
no longer authentically live. I do
not choke on pure baptismal water,
I, breathless, jaw-dropped from the ultra awe
arise from the Heaven-white waves, whipping
my head, born anew, in the arms of the Saint
who fully embraces me, who leads me shoreward

then states: "you are born anew, and, now ..."
while she raises her upturned hands I
levitate a foot above the pool—
I dripping like one who has only known water;
I dripping like one who's known air the first time;
I feeling just the pinch of water-fall mist,
I knowing that, henceforth, I must do
the will of God, alone, unmingled with
my own; and surrender to Him, alone,
speaking only when He opens my mouth
with His voice, alone, when He explodes me
into Scripture, any-where, or newly-
refracts His orders through me, from Heaven.
I dripping like one who has only known water,
I dripping like one who's known air the first time,
and, now, I'm whirling clock-wise, my addictions,
my lusts, my vices, my illness
—all these leeches of my vital essence—
rent from me. I feel no more wrath.
My face is strain-free as a baby's.
I feel Dante feeling what I'm feeling:
the lightness of spirit that soars a seraphim.
I slowly, downwardly float toward
the water, after which I reunite
with Dante Alighieri on
the rocks, once more, wherefrom we see
the Maid of Orleans fade into the air
of an unindifferent Universe. "So,
now, do you see the contradictions of
the two seditions that you birthed and raised?
Yes, Padrino. My slate-clean spirit's

only wish is to light-speedily spread God's
word, and only God's word, O Titan!
While catching full sight of a fast-falling star
blazing inside my periphery, Dante
disappears ... Outside the flaming Century
Manor, where the patients are winning
the battle for its massive patio,
Flavia, with a wide birch-bough,
rams the Manor's northern door. I
tackle Flavia into high bushes, hiding
us both from the enemies. "What
the fuck are you doing, comrade?!
Flav, we must *wave the white flag*
now—surrender our forces, lest our souls
be dashed by the Almighty's wrath! I know
this all must sound so dense, but we must wave
the white flag; do you understand, comrade?
Faced down, Flavia thrashes frenziedly,
but cannot break away from me. Through her
iPhone I order a full surrender
despite the oncoming victory.
Soon, no more roars, nor shots, nor battle-
cries, just the march of oncoming officers
shining bright lights into the high bushes.

XXI. A Letter from Flavia Vamorri

from: | Flavia Vamorri <bakuninite.2000@gmail.com> |

to: | Crito Di Volta <san.francisco.ave@gmail.com> |

I'm spent.

I'm 'completely given,' Crito.

I think you should break your house arrest the first chance you get; you are no longer safe.

Like Dante said, don't mingle the words of the Lord with your own. Only speak when spoken through.

Crito, I can't … Crito—I'm going.

The failure of my mission, the PTSD, the limitless mania, the infinite depression, the pointless fluctuations, the stiff stupors, the emotionless psychiatrists, the endless torment, the blatant incurability, the infinite stigmas, the ultimate failure, the bottomless bitterness, are all too much for me now.

Yours,

Flavia

XXII. After the Funeral

Passing a fire in a park without lamps,
the wind upwhirls a gray bouquet to me
from the open hearth of legendary tramps
whose cans I fill with heirloom jewellery.

I climb up a yew in the shade of a soul
waltzing to his whistling, free.
A beggar-girl sings with every toll
of church-bells pounding my heart for me.

These past ward-mates of mine now throng.
I finger my rope like a rosary bead.
My people will leave when the fire is dead.
"I'm just up here to see the view—I'm fine!"

I feign my strongest gaze to the skyline ...

XXIII. The Affirmation

I. *piccolo sonetto*

Still in sublimely blissful
surprise, I arrive at Flavia's
viridian veranda,
then faintly tap a single

pentameter against
the very door by which she'd
speed past to greet her
pre-dawns. She'd sip

the dew that dripped from her brow
like invigorating wine,
when, amid fantastic

shadows, she'd start to strum
her wounded shoe-strings' elastics like
a lyre, one foot near her heart.

II.

11:11 a.m.

After Flavia's father, dressed in black, welcomes me into the Vamorri home, Flavia's mother—looking beauteous as ever, despite her most dismal hours, and also dressed in black—funereally steps herself down the stairs, then brokenly embraces me.

Alberto leads us into the kitchen. Gemma and I sit across from each other at the kitchen table, but then, fully realizing the width of the table and the distance between us, I arise; I sit next to her before a closed window through which a sunless, dying white birch stands amid blows of the whipping wind. Alberto begins to make coffee.

III.

Last night, I begin, *at 1:11 a.m., while in my bedroom, I begged Flavia, on my knees, in unfathomably grievous prayer: "Speak to me, please! O let me know you're de facto immortal, as I have faith! Give me a sign, my comrade, my love!" As I arose, I felt a breath-taking presence that unexplainably advised me to close my eyes—then, my eyes, under their lids, witnessed a whirlwind of two white balls of light fantastically waltzing. Upon being advised by the presence to open my eyes, I heard behind me a piece of paper descending from the ceiling. And, lo and behold, upon the floor: the program I had received at her funeral—the program I had been carrying, like a holy relic, in the left breast pocket of my blazer, which, upon inspection, was*

now empty! At that moment I knew—not believed, but knew—
that Flavia Vamorri was in the room; and soon expressed to me,
not with language, but through what may have been electro-
magnetic projections, that she loves me, that she loves you, that
her soul lives on ... Suddenly, Talk Talk's extended version of "It's
My Life" flourished from my MacBook Air like an audible
flower, and so we danced, my eyes now open, she leading—my
body with her soul, my mind with her body, my soul with her
mind; until, finally, my soul with her soul, we danced, I all the
while weeping tears of measureless relief, of utmost joy. We jived
and jived and jived. Then she communicated to me: "Crito Di
Volta, never enable my ending to kill you—otherwise I die a
second death. Never enable my ending to kill you—I wish to
live forever in your verse. Never enable my ending to kill
you—forever in your verse; fulfill my last wish."

"Do you know the lyrics of the song?" implores Gemma.
Yes.
"Why don't you sing it for us, Crito?"
Gemma and Alberto heard me sing House of the Rising
Sun, once, at a karaoke party for Flavia's nineteenth birthday.
I clear my throat.

IV.

While I sing the coda, a flash of white light explodes
from behind me, but I continue singing towards the final
note of the song. I see Gemma and Alberto suddenly transfix
their thoroughly startled eyes upon something behind me.

The song now sung, their wide-open eyes seem to break from a trance. I turn around to find nothing extraordinary behind me, but rather, a large, empty, nineteenth century silver frame, hanging on the red wall of the next room.

What's going on, guys?

"Crito, while you were singing, light began beaming from the empty frame, which once held the Liam Gallagher painting you gifted Flavia on her birthday. After the failure of the uprising, she felt betrayed by you, so she removed the painting from the frame, which she inherited from her grandmother on Alberto's side." Gemma says.

"Crito, did you know that Flavia even painted that room red just so it would match the painting?" asks Alberto.

"She loved that painting so much," continues Gemma. "So, after the white rays of light scattered from the painting—and I mean this completely, and I mean this literally—Flavia, with her hair the very color of the room, appeared inside the frame, smiling at us with tears flowing down her smiling face. She mouthed: "I love you," but did not make a sound. After an unexplainable calm entered my heart, she disappeared from the frame. Then, your painting of Liam Gallagher appeared inside the frame.

"This was my experience, too!" Alberto exclaims.

Gemma and Alberto embrace like two calming, warming zephyrs.

XXIV. Holy Lyrics

I. *The Voice That I Have Heard In Recent Dreams*

"The Stranger now saddles me into my bliss.
I wear the rising sun at my heart's core.
White roses bloom beneath the supernovae.
If I should stir a sleeping alley-beggar
on my wind-backed way, I may give
him a glimpse of his daydream's Paradise
while our opening eyes might soon meet through
the wintry winds of this late summer dawn.
I feel the Stranger's whip now heal me.
I *am* the dew-bowed one who flings
his eye-light while he sings; who strayed
his white way blazing forth like one light-beam;
who hung with the waifs and the whores
and the lepers, the touched-with-fire
maniacal, in the black eye-black night;
who hung with Peter in the twilight of
the dawn of Götterdämmerung,
whose bright white wrists conduct the wisps
of salamander cirruses, up in rightly skies.
His wrath is wrought and wrung throughout my hands,
yet I'm not asking you to worship me
nor give me your coat; I do not care what you
can do for me. I need no love but my own
Father's love, yet in the End, O in the End,

just walk beside me and be my friend,
just walk beside me and be my friend
and, now, take His wrath and love with my long sword
of light, my kiss of sky and sea meeting
upon thee, my dew-balmed lips not quavering,
no, but rising with His vermillion greeting—
And I, like a falcon, judge the game
beneath me, the act of humankind;
and I down-circle on some, yet I,
of course leave alone the others who are
saved, still, and some to be eternally.
The Stranger steers me while I veer you toward
the Vortex of Utopia, the Era of Ease.
Will you fight the draw of my Father's breath?
Reach Mount Zion by Götterdämmerung?
Silkily down-spiral like some funeral lilies?!"

II. *While Begging Under February Stars*

While begging under February stars
that I might be my closest to the beggars
and scatter my soul through the forecasted storm
and brave them on toward the laze and warm
of spring, a stinging wind ascended and engraved
in my ear the whimper of a girl I had saved
from her own hand, inside her freshman dorm;
then nursed, at once, from her childhood wars.
She whispered, "please reverse the weather in my
eyes," empty as two open sunless graves,
which simply realigned the little troth
I'd sided for the sewing of my wounds;
back to the Father and the snow then falling
on the woman in my arms, no longer calling.

III. *The Wool-White Slow Light Snow Falls On The Street*

The wool-white slow light snow falls on the street
of this stepless city's windless alleyway,
where I stand tomb-still to hear my heart beat,

my back against a church, my trail-blazed feet
blistered by universal searches through the day;
the wool-white slow light snow falls on the street

as soft as Dymphna's fingers fall on meat-
less shoulders of the girl I overhear pray,
where I stand tomb-still to hear my heart beat

while she brokenly begs to the Lord, in the heat,
and not to the horde, in the cold, where she'll stay,
where wool-white slow light snow falls on the street,

where I could die tonight and feel complete,
where every moment feels like bonus-pay,
where I stand tomb-still and hear my heart beat,

where I will wait for her, so we might meet—
where I might give all she will take, then stray.
The wool-white slow light snow falls on the street
where I stand tomb-still to hear my heart beat.

IV. *To See The Faces of The Father And The Son*

To see the faces of the Father and the Son
first turn your back on your own reflection,
then burn your ego by the magnified beams
of your soul eclipsed by the moon of your dreams—
dreams of a bondage we are programmed to love blind,
while cheerleading the destruction of our kind.

V. *When One Esteems ...*

When one esteems one's
reputation in Heaven
more than one's reputation
on earth, one's soul,

a-sudden, transmutes
from still-born blue
cocoon to white-winged
butterfly birth.

One must prize
one's reputation in the Creator's
heart, more than one's reputation

in His creations' eyes,
to ensure a place in, or any-
where near, His Paradise.

VI. *Do You See What I See? Do You See What I See?*

Do you see what I see? Do you see what I see?
A star, a star, dancing in the night,
and a world blinded by its twilight?
Do you hear what I hear? Do you hear what I hear?
Or have you been detuned from the Voice
I clearly hear (Do you have a choice?)
and replaced His daily winking signs
with hypnosis-casting media-screens—
replaced the Son whose sword will soon spell danger
for those who jeer Him in these in-betweens,
who make these in-betweens of lives their deaths,
who turn the Personal Jesus into a Stranger …
Born before my star-high bar, I am not sorry
for trying to make my life, and yours, gallops of glory!

VII. *Three Emile Nelligan Translations*

A   *Christ on the Cross*

I'd always gaze into this plaster Jesus
pitched like a pardon at the old abbey-door—
a black-gestured, solemn scaffold;
with saintly idolatry I'd bow before.

Now as I sat around, at the hour of cricket's play,
in funereal fields, blue-viewedly musing,
one near-past night with wind-blown hair, reciting
Eloa, in that swelled esthetic, ephebic way,

I noticed near the debris of a wall
the heavy old cross heaped up tall
and crumbled plaster among primroses;

and I froze, doleful, with pensive eyes,
and heard spasmodic hammers strike, in me,
the black spikes of my own Calvary!

B   *Response from the Cross*

While dying on Golgotha's bloody boughs,
which grief engulfed you most, O Nazarene?
The grief of hearing Father say and mean:
'Now sleep to keep the last of all your vows'?

When the funeral choir lamented without You,
and nails ripped your palms; when, on a plain,
your spirit scattered the flower of its breath,
surpassing your flight to Celestial States—

Lord, what was that sigh of ceaseless dearth
you exhaled when your mission was complete,
when you began to consider your next feat?

Will you reveal to me this mystery?
"Child, I was grieving the truth—that I
would never hug my executioners on earth."

C   *Small Stained-Glass Window*

Blond-bearded Jesus, with eyes of soft sapphire,
smiles in an ancient stained-glass window choir,
amid the sacred flight of singing cherubim,
who look to Him—to listen to Him, to love Him.
The birds of Zion, with wings of clarity and calm,
are in the sun whose dust-grains flash like wild-fire,
and it's sweet as a master's song on the lyre
to see them so, among the arabesques of palm,
in this small stained-glass window where sunbeams dim
amid the sacred flight of singing cherubim.
And smiling with mystical kindness behind the choir,
Christ, with golden beard and eyes of soft sapphire.

XXV. Holy Thursday

I.

Elora is that town where Amos goes to espy an Edenic Dimension beyond the third. The Greyhound bus manoeuvres through the Guelph University cabstand as naturally as water through the banks of a winding stream. Giddy Amos awaits me with a widely smile while the flawless Holy Thursday sunbeams scatter for as long as forever is.

Amos!

I blare like a siren through the open, tinted window.

Inside his pearl white, sixty-nine Benz—it belonged to his passed-on father figure, Leonard Cohen–we cruise from the cabstand toward that town whose name means, "God is Light," in Hebraic; then, from brown, dilapidated farms, to white, still-standing horses; from relentlessly lingering wasps we fail to out-speed, to new mountain wheat waving divinely in the distance.

II.

"D'ya like Rachmaninoff's Prelude in C?"

That would suit me perfectly.

"Do you miss rock n' roll? How long have you gone without it now?

Like, weeks. No withdrawal, either.

Amos presses play.

"Should we further our Yeshua-pertaining fire-exchanges ignited on the phone last night?"

Let's.

"Well, I'll begin with a refrain: Jesus of Nazareth, simply stated, did not fulfil the messianic prophecies of the Old Testament—and maybe you're beginning to see that?"

I look gently but firmly into his eyes.

We're driving down a newly paved hill. I do not respond —not in a passive-aggressive, half-combative way, but as an anti-action from which could plausibly spring the waters of some acquiescence from the fountains of our presently magmatic spirits, *regardless of* our opposing opinions.

"Jesus," Amos continues, "did *not* glean my Jewish Brethren from their exile, nor lead them toward Israel—nor did he rebuild the Temple in Jerusalem, did he, my brother? … I'd advance to say that Jesus of Nazareth, or Yeshua, or whoever may have been born wherever, and at whatever time, did *not* fulfill those Old Testament prophecies. Crito, you say Jesus healed a blind man in the Temple, yet can you even slightly prove this? You say he was born under particular stars, that he was born of the Virgin Mary, yet how, again, can you confirm this? Did the Nazarene birth *any* peace on this damned earth? Look, mang—in short, if the Nazarene were indeed the Christ, why do we still have wars, famine, genocide, epidemics, etcetera."

Jesus was indeed out-casted by his own people; and yet, indeed, was the light that spread to all the ends of the earth … Among the Jews of History, Jesus of Nazareth, alone, fits the

Saviour's description, doesn't He? And did the Nazarene not shepherd living spirits toward the Father by way of faith in the Father's Son? And did He not drive living spirits toward their sins' forgiveness by the way of faith in this Yeshua?

"Wait. Surely you see: all you say is built on the sands of human testimony," Amos says.

Yes, it was *human testimony, yet this human testimony is vast and everywhere throughout the world—a divine sign in itself.*

We pull into the Elora parkette, with benches beside tulips, with wide views of the gray-yellow Grand River flowing toward what end on earth I'll never know, despite strong hypotheses; for now, all I need to know is that the Grand River flows. Here we stand, as straight as our intentions for the other, while a setting sun flings crimson over blissful-seeming yachted waters.

"All this we're talking about—it seems quite solvable to me," Amos starts. "When, like a white bolt of lightning hitting its rod, or like a sword piercing through a curtain, the true Messiah, at last, awe-strikes human eyes for the first time—breath-takes human lungs for the first time—and, then, thereafter, assuredly fulfills this, that, and the other Old Testament prophecies, unlike Jesus of Nazareth, I pray I am there."

III.

O, Amos, listen, know: I contend with you about the Messiah, not to spark an irreverence between us, *but to spark*

a revelation within you—*something like the revelation you
sparked, in me, regarding electricity, the cartilage of the Universe!
… Now, Listen!*

My speech is intruded by out-of-nowhere cardinal
wha-cheers comingling with mourning dove coo-ahs.

*You say it is simple: the Messiah will come and this, that,
and the other, must transpire; but here is where your speech may
be flawed.*

*See: nowhere in the Bible do the prophets present the
Messianic duties the way you say.*

*See: we must ceaselessly read the Old Testament as closely as
our own eyes are to their own visions; since, nowhere in the Old
Testament is there a specific, categorical list, which was, in fact,
an afterthought not conceived until the Middle Ages by Moses
Maimonides.*

In the Talmud too, one can not *find such a list of Messianic
duties lain out like you say.*

Amos' visage is paroxysmal but still exudes warmth.

IV.

"Now, listen, if there was expectation that the Son of
God would come before the Second Temple was destroyed,
and if the Temple was still standing in His lifetime, *how*
could He rebuild it?!"

Amos hauls on his Marlboro Red.

But the Bible does not *outright identify specific passages as
Messianic. It doesn't ever say: 'lo, the following passage is a*

messianic prophecy, and it is indisputable.' So, see, you believe the Christ will, in what I would consider His Second Coming, re-gather all the Jews in exile, re-build the Temple, and destroy all wickedness from the earth; and, see, these are all the feats he will *achieve! Let us say, for the sake of argument, that there are thirty-three so-called Old Testament prophecies. It is as though you think the Saviour will immediately go from one to thirty-three, in his fulfilling of so-called explicit Old Testament prophecies. Is it that, in your mind, Jesus has realized prophecies one to sixteen, but because he did not complete seventeen to thirty-three, he cannot plausibly be the Messiah? So, the Christ must self-sacrificially die for all our sins, must rise from the dead, must fling the light and word of God to the ends of the earth, etcetera, etcetera; and He must to do all this before the Second Temple was destroyed ... There is only* one *possible candidate, here a candidate that may remotely resemble the Saviour, and that is Jesus of Nazareth. And when He returns to live out the rest of the prophecies, and there is no more doubt of who He is, there will no longer be time for your faith!*

Amos, you believe that Jesus could not have been the Christ because here we are, still, in this endless Emergency Present, fighting countless wars, dying in ghastly famines, and the Jews are still scattered, and the Temple is not risen. But, I ask with all my love: who was the one who clearly executed the tasks that most needed executing, two thousand years ago? We have a good, even logical, hope that He will *return again, and fulfil the rest of his duties! We have* more *than a good hope! Do you not remotely feel the Lord's assurance in your spirit, O AMOS?! Do you hear me?*

V.

See, those who deny the Nazarene hold no hope, since the Redeemer's duties, in their mind, which had to happen, already, has not *happened; yet, I refrain, do we not have good reason to believe that He will, at last, fulfil prophecies seventeen to thirty-three, seeing He has already fulfilled one to sixteen!? And when He returns to live out the rest of the prophecies, and there is no more doubt of who He is, there will no longer be time for your faith, as I have said! O Amos! Do not be forever damned.*

I know you know *I've verily expressed myself, here, in your virgin Elora, because of an unconditional love for you who once saved me. Please, never—never forget that.*

"I *will never* forget the love you have beamed here, today, Crito, a love as rightly as the sun that rays upon us; and I will *never* forget your utmost loyalty; and I will forever ponder your word-flourishes flowering in my ear today.

But pondering will not be enough!

After moments of silence I assert:

You must follow me, my leader.

While striding toward the mast-white sands of the shimmering Elora shore, I hear Amos' footfalls behind me until we reach the near-deserted beach. I kneel and shape some sand while Amos remains standing, his hand on hip.

"And this Holy Spirit, *where* is it? Is it from without or within?"

Dare I answer your question?

"What do you mean? What are you doing there?"

I continue to sculpt.

"Wow, that's extraordinary, Crito. I never knew you could—O my God, is that a—"

I uplift into the air the white dove of sand that forthwith transmutes into a white dove of flesh fluttering and caressing Amos' face, his eyes as open as his jaw. The white dove of flesh then turns to the White Dove of the Holy Spirit, whose eyes beam hyper-light through Amos' pupils—his face, for the first time, tensionless as a baby's—then, a-sudden, the White Dove light-speedily departs toward the riven heavens, while Amos throws himself upon the beach, then kneels next to me, astonished.

XXVI. A Letter to Amos Heine

from: | *Crito Di Volta <san.francisco.ave@gmail.com>* |

to: | *Amos Heine <the.montreal.prize@gmail.com>* |

Dear Amos,

I have painted "The Crucifixion" for you.

I have penned you "The Voice That I Have Heard," at the insistences of the Lord Himself.

Whose voice that I have heard I do not know. Do you?

Love,

Crito

The Voice That I Have Heard in Recent Dreams

for Amos Heine

"My spirit is an open city now.
The minute-men of my last fight are dead.
My last-born Hope is shot inside her bed.
My nape of Faith now takes a bloody bow
before the scattering sides of the war:
the Stranger and the humankind, who stoke
His heart with my dying hand, choke
my ministers, then open my red scar.
I feel my memories flood the streets
like children after fire-testing bells—
and I'm gone ... I am now the morning star;
my centre burns for you though I'm so far.
And though you mar my name now, I am still
your guide. Forgiving you is my last will."

XXVII. Holy Thursday Evening

I.

Since I was born again I have not sinned
in ways that might endanger my salvation,
—or so I believe—and the Father transmits
to me the messages of light I see
entirely enter the newly-cleansed Temple
of my essence, whose sun-roof's clear as
the First Commandment. I speak none other
than His words on soap-boxes throughout the city.
Now, an on-coming student—O, it's
Laura—the girl with the camouflaged shirt
who passed up cool spring water to me
while I blasted on the sky-blue table top
at McMaster University. I've not
seen Laura since that jangle at the Flat Rock
with the many masked men of the Tandem.
As we pass each other at the intersection
she smiles and shares her warm, naive touch—
then pulls a pistol from her purse, then shoves
me into an awaiting hearse. "Shut the fuck
up and calm the fuck down, or this
will be a ride you won't survive," mutters
the driver. My hands are cuffed
before me while I'm blind-folded. I ride
with faithfulness, with readiness, with peace,

while we speed toward "this warehouse, Crito,"
says the driver, "much like the warehouse in
Tarantino's *Reservoir Dogs*."

II.

Bright movie-lights illume a tall
crookedly standing cross, a wall of blood
and brains, and a guillotine, at the West
end of the Warehouse; where men and women
with whips and chains and maces await me.
In the East end of the Warehouse:
militaristic, sullen drumming.
A Tandemite removes his mask—
It's Bruno Grunn! It's Bruno Grunn! "Crito,
you have much to offer what you've called
the Unholy Tandem. Will you
live and die by the First Commandment?
Crito Di Volta, repeat after me:
 "Jesus of Nazareth was not the Christ;
Jesus of Nazareth is excrement."
Jesus of Nazareth … Jesus of Nazareth was—
Jesus of Nazareth was indeed *the Christ!*
Jesus of Nazareth is perfection!
"Very well, then," Bruno coldly states.
"While your tormentors prepare their maces
of iron, their whips of steel, a last
wish? *Remove my shackles and cuffs, then*
allow me some moments to pray and pen

inside my diary. "Okay," Bruno
says, "but you won't know when we will stop
you; there is no timer on these 'moments'."

III.

O Lord who stands on air in Heaven,
hearing this prayer, suffer the coals
of their souls into diamonds, if this be
the only way they may fall their
closest to Your glory, these ones who
are presently blind to their own spirits.
O Son who stands on air in Heaven,
hearing this prayer, take these diamonds
freely, on Judgement Day—freely as You
died for all their sins—freely as so many, still,
will mock You, but soon will mock no more!
O Holy Spirit, in the air of the world,
hearing this prayer, when this sentence
is complete, enter those whose minds can
not discern their souls in the Twilight.

O Lord who stands on air in Heaven, hearing
this prayer, bring me bravery and thunder,
tonight, that I may vivaciously
die for You with roars rather than whimpers.
Help me to die like a lion, even if I am a lamb.
O Lord who stands on air in Heaven, hearing
this prayer, tell me who and what I am

before I face the maces. I feel traces
of the poltergeists enslaved inside
this place, yet I am calm and unafraid.
Explosions of light burst behind my head,
casting, outside the warehouse, images
of my life; and, too, explosions of light
burst from beyond the warehouse, casting,
upon the warehouse ceiling, silhouettes
of familiar faces—Niccolo's visage exploded above me ...
glass shatters ... and O! O! O
Lord who stands on air in Heaven, hearing
this prayer, I cry through bloody eyes, yet, at last, can see! ...
O humankind revolving like a gyre—
O martyrs before me who challenged the fire—
O those of you who'll come and up-stand—
at last I know just who and what I am:

Acknowledgments

"A Letter To Flavia Vamorri" first appeared in *Crito Di Volta (I-IV; VII and XII),* published by Frog Hollow Press, 2015.

"A Letter To Niccolo Di Volta," lines 9-12 of *Jesus and Judas* from Charles Baudelaire's "Gypsies' Journey," translated by Marc and Carlo Di Saverio.

"Standing On Opposite Sides of the Stream" first appeared in *the Fiddlehead Magazine, 2018.*

"New Year's" first appeared in *Crito Di Volta (I-IV, VII and XII),* published by Frog Hollow Press, 2015.

"Prelude to the Overpoet" first appeared in *Canadian Notes and Queries Magazine,* Spring 2015.

"Dare We, Dare We, Now" first published as "Ode to my Discoverer" in *the Fiddlehead Magazine*, 2018.

In Part III of "Orphomusocracy," lines 1-12 of quatrains from Gerard de Nerval's "Golden Sonnet," translated by Carlo and Marc Di Saverio, 2002.

In part III of "Orphomusocracy," from "Niccolo booms with ardour," to "For example, the endings of songs today are usually their beginnings," researched and composed by Paul Di Saverio.

"Page 1: Phonetoverse," first appeared in *Sanatorium Songs* (2013).

"Objectverse Photograph" first appeared in *Sanatorium Songs: a chapbook* (2010), and was originally composed in 2006.

"The Paralytic" first appeared in *Hamilton Arts and Letters Magazine, 2019.*

"Une Chanson D'Amour D'un Esthete Cyclothmique" first
    appeared in *Crito Di Volta (I-IV, VII and XII),* published
    by Frog Hollow Press, 2015.

    "G" first appeared in *Partisan Magazine,* 2016.

"Il Mortarista 2" was inspired by *Thunderbolts of the Gods*
    (a movie from 2012 based on a book by the same name,
    which was originally published in 2005 and written by
    Wallace Thornhill and David Talbott).

In Part III of "Il Mortarista 2" lines 9-92 composed by Asa
    Boxer and Marc di Saverio.

In "A Visitation" lines 11-22 from Victor Segalen's "Bad
    Craftsmen" translated by Marc and Carlo Di Saverio.

Part III of "A Visitation" largely based on/derived from my
    interview with Laura Furster, who synthesized "The
    Language of Madness," an article first appearing in the
    Hamilton Spectator in November, 2017.

"A Translation of "Canto I" from Dante's *Inferno,"* translated
    by Marc and Carlo Di Saverio, first appeared in *The Secular
    Heretic Magazine* (Summer 2019).

Emile Nelligan's "On a Portrait of Dante," lines 29-42
    translated by Carlo and Marc Di Saverio.

"Holy Lyrics Part VII," translated by Carlo and Marc
    Di Saverio.

"The Voice that I Have Heard" first appeared as "Citta
    Aperta" in Carousel Magazine, 2017.

Quote from back cover, "[*Crito Di Volta*] exceeds Allen
    Ginsberg's *Howl* in both authenticity and intensity," by
    Symon Jory Stevens-Guille.

There are so many family members, friends and colleagues
I would like to thank, and personally address, below; however,
because of time restrictions, I will be unable to thank and
personally address so many who have encouraged me along
the way of writing *Crito*. Please know: I remember you,
I thank you, and I love you.

For now, I wish to thank: the Living God, the Almighty
Creator of All, under whose direction I wrote this book;
the late but unforgettable Michelle Fabris, who inspired
and emboldened me to write *Crito*; and this poem's saving
grace, Anna van Valkenburg, my supernatural editor.

Finally, I would like to thank the truly limitless and
extraordinary Guernica Editions for publishing this book.

About the Author

MARC DI SAVERIO hails from Hamilton, Canada.
His poems and translations have appeared internationally.
In Issue 92 of Canadian Notes and Queries Magazine, di
Saverio's *Sanatorium Songs* (2013) was hailed as "the greatest
poetry debut from the past 25 years." In 2016 he received the
City of Hamilton Arts Award for Best Emerging Writer. In
2017, his work was broadcasted on BBC Radio 3, his debut
became a best seller in both Canada and the United States,
and he published his first book of translations: *Ship of Gold:
The Essential Poems of Emile Nelligan* (Vehicule Press).
He is currently writing his first novel, *The Daymaker*.